Test, train, affirm & send into ministry:

Recovering the local church's responsibility in the external call

Brian Croft

DayOne

©Day One Publications 2010
First printed 2010

Scripture quotations taken from the New American Standard Bible®, Copyright © 1960, 1962, 1963, 1968, 1971, 1972, 1973, 1975, 1977, 1995 by The Lockman Foundation. Used by permission. (www.Lockman.org)

A CIP record is held at the British Library

ISBN 978-1-84625-197-9

Published by Day One Publications, Ryelands Road, Leominster, HR6 8NZ
☎ 01568 613 740
FAX 01568 611 473
email—sales@dayone.co.uk
web site—www.dayone.co.uk
North American e-mail—usasales@dayone.co.uk
North American web site—www.dayonebookstore.com

Cover designed by Wayne McMaster and printed in the USA

Dedication
To the saints of Auburndale Baptist Church,
who, by their selfless and sacrificial willingness,
powerfully model this responsibility to send out
those among us whom we dearly love for the
sake of Christ's church and the glory of God.

And to my brother Scott, who first challenged
me to seek and value the external call.

ENDORSEMENTS

We live in an individualistic world where subjective and private experiences are often thought to be beyond contradiction. If someone claims that he is called to ministry, who are we to doubt it? Brian Croft demonstrates, however, that an internal call to ministry must be matched by an external call. The people of God, the church of Jesus Christ, should play a major role in assessing whether someone is called to ministry. Croft's book is biblically grounded and full of wise pastoral advice. I commend it enthusiastically.

Thomas R. Schreiner, James Buchanan Harrison Professor of New Testament Interpretation, Southern Baptist Theological Seminary, USA

Brian Croft loves the Savior, and he loves the church. That comes through in every page of this book. And every page of this book offers cogent, biblical, and useful instruction for this most necessary of responsibilities in the local church: testing, training, affirming, and sending workers into the ministry. For those of us who care that the harvest is plentiful and want the Lord of the harvest to send workers, this book helps us to be sure the workers are worth their wages. Croft tells us what to look for, and when we find it, how to cultivate it.

Thabiti Anyabwile, Senior Pastor, First Baptist Church of Grand Cayman, Cayman Islands, and author, What Is a Healthy Church Member?

The church possesses a unique responsibility to identify leaders among God's people and equip them for ministry among all peoples. As the Holy Spirit sets men apart for ministry, the local community of faith is accountable to God for training them up and sending them out in a way that glorifies Christ. I am thankful to Brian Croft for this immensely helpful, thoroughly biblical, and extremely practical resource that will serve those called by God, their pastors, and their churches well.

David Platt, Senior Pastor, The Church at Brook Hills, Birmingham, Alabama, USA

Brian Croft provides clear, practical teaching about the role of the local church regarding men who sense a call to vocational ministry. This process used to be referred to as a church's ongoing ministry of "calling out the called." Pastor Croft has led his church to develop an intentional approach to evaluating a man's sense of call, an approach that is as effective as that of almost any church I know. If you have responsibilities of spiritual leadership in your local church, you'll want to get this book, for you'll find it helpful every time a man indicates that he senses God's call to vocational ministry.

Donald Whitney, Associate Professor of Biblical Spirituality and former Director of Applied Ministry, Southern Baptist Theological Seminary, USA

Filled with sound theology and practical wisdom, this well-organized guide will fill a gap on pastors' bookshelves. This is the resource that many churches and ministers have long needed to help them fulfill their God-given roles in evaluating those who consider themselves called to the ministry. One can only imagine the blessing for the Lord's church as local congregations implement the methods described in this necessary little book.

Jackson Boyett, Pastor, Dayspring Chapel, Austin, Texas, and Chairman of the Board, To Every Tribe Ministries, USA

When Paul wrote to the Galatians he expected those churches to be able to discern whether the true gospel was being preached or whether what they were hearing was another (no-) gospel—even if the preacher was Paul himself or an angel from heaven! This book calls churches to take up responsibilities Paul expected them to exercise, and pastors to do the kind of work Paul charged Timothy and Titus to do. May the Lord use it to equip pastors and congregations to raise up those whom the Holy Spirit will make overseers, pastors, and elders for the good of God's people and the glory of his name.

> **Jim Hamilton, Associate Professor of Biblical Theology, Southern Baptist Theological Seminary, and Senior Pastor, Kenwood Baptist Church, Louisville, Kentucky, USA**

Brian's first book, Visit the Sick, is a gift to pastors and local churches alike. Theologically rich and skillful in equipping, it has served myself and the pastors I labor alongside. In Test, Train, Affirm & Send into Ministry, Brian delivers again. Here's much-needed biblical discernment for ordinary pastors (like myself). Pastor, read it to benefit your soul. Read it to equip your church. Read it to be amazed that you serve the Chief Shepherd.

> **Brian Chesemore, Pastor of Family Life Covenant Life Church, Gaithersburg, Maryland, USA**

Brian Croft's book, Test, Train, Affirm & Send into Ministry, provides an alternate opinion to the pervasive concept of "calling" into the ministry. Croft highlights the necessity of the church's responsibility to execute the external call to or affirm individuals who claim a personal divine draw to the ministry. This perspective undermines the highly individualistic, exclusive, almost Gnostic sense of call that people speak about *today and which is automatically considered above evaluation or critique from anyone, let alone the local church. This book will start lots of conversations and change some minds about how we as the body of Christ, particularly in the Low Church tradition, affirm the pastoral ministry of individuals. Thank you, Pastor Croft, for contributing to this important conversation!*

D. Jeffrey Mooney, Senior Pastor, First Baptist Church, Norco, California, and Assistant Professor of Old Testament Interpretation and Theology, California Baptist University, USA

As a pastor and pastoral-ministries instructor, I greatly enjoyed this work! What Brian Croft has written will help pastors, churches, seminary professors and students include an important but often missed step in a man's journey from a mysterious call to the ministry to a local congregation's call of that man to a pastorate. Brian's challenge rightly returns the responsibility of laying hands on a pastoral candidate from the academy to the local congregation and its elders, while also calling church leaders to recover a proper concept of "no man suddenly" within the affirmation process—one that is gospel-promoting in its intentionality, discernment, investments, and length. Vocational and lay leaders should keep this work close at hand when a man professes an inward call to ministry. May its truths help to strengthen the body of Christ with biblically based appointments of God-fearing, Spirit-called, elder-trained, and church-affirmed shepherds of the flock of God.

Eric C. Redmond, Senior Pastor, Reformation Alive Baptist Church, Temple Hills, and Assistant Professor of Bible and Theology and of Pastoral Ministries, Washington Bible College, Lanham, Maryland, USA

The importance of pastoral affirmation cannot be overstated. Much of the health of our local churches rises and falls on such a weighty matter. Brian Croft has helpfully heralded a call to local churches to return to the ownership of pastoral discipleship. This work will offer great clarity where much confusion has been found in recent years.

Eric Bancroft, Senior Pastor, Castleview Baptist Church, Indianapolis, Indiana, and Former Adjunct Professor, The Master's College, USA

In this new and important book, Brian Croft presents a bold and biblical understanding of the call to ministry. Along the way, Brian clarifies many issues of contemporary confusion, and his commitment to the local church ensures that his understanding of the call to ministry is never severed from the context of God's people. Few books are more timely than this one, and I am thankful to Brian Croft for his faithful and careful consideration of the call to ministry.

R. Albert Mohler, Jr., President, The Southern Baptist Theological Seminary

ACKNOWLEDGMENTS

A special thanks to:

Matt Crawford, Jason Adkins, Adam Embry, and Greg Van Court, for your friendship, gospel partnership, and willingness to exercise your gifts to improve immensely the clarity and content of this project. Your effort to serve me in this way in the midst of your busy schedules was both humbling and inspiring.

Day One Publications, for seeing the value in this work and your continued support; and especially Jim Holmes, for your friendship, partnership, excitement, and encouragement through this project.

Dr. Mohler, for your kind and encouraging words contained in the Foreword of this book and your constant prodding of the local church to assume the training of pastors and missionaries.

The faithful saints of Auburndale Baptist Church, who allow me the gift of your fellowship, the encouragement of your love, and your endless support of my labor in the Word for the sake of your souls. You model the selflessness required to give up those among us who have been called.

My elder brother, Scott, who many years ago loved me enough to challenge my calling when unaccompanied by the affirmation of others. Since then you have remained a wise counselor, inspiring example, and beloved friend to me.

My children: Samuel, Abby, Isabelle, and Claire. What unspeakable joy you bring me by your love, care, and affection! You remain a daily example to me of God's undeserved goodness and grace.

My wife, who remained steadfast in love, encouragement, and support through the approaching deadlines and late nights of writing. Apart from my Savior, there is no one I love more or find more joy in than you.

Our Chief Shepherd, who empowers his shepherds to faithfully shepherd his people until his glorious appearing (1 Peter 5:1–4).

CONTENTS

FOREWORD **12**

PREFACE **14**

INTRODUCTION **16**

1 PROLOGUE: TO WHAT IS THE PASTOR CALLED? **18**

2 WHO IS RESPONSIBLE FOR THE EXTERNAL CALL? **30**

3 WHO SHOULD RECEIVE THE EXTERNAL CALL? **38**

4 WHO GIVES THE EXTERNAL CALL? **50**

5 HOW SHOULD WE PROCEED WITH THE EXTERNAL CALL? **60**

6 WHAT IS AT STAKE WITH THE EXTERNAL CALL? **72**

7 CONCLUSION **80**

APPENDIX 1 PASTORAL INTERNSHIP TEMPLATE **86**

APPENDIX 2 SERVICE REVIEW EVALUATION **89**

APPENDIX 3 THE EXTERNAL CALL (ACTS 13:1–3) **92**

ENDNOTES **103**

FOR FURTHER HELP AND INFORMATION **105**

FOREWORD

Has God called you to ministry? Though all Christians are called to serve the cause of Christ, God calls certain persons to serve the church as pastors and other ministers. The Apostle Paul affirmed that if a man aspires to be a pastor, "it is a fine work he aspires to do" (1 Tim. 3:1, NASB). Likewise, it is a high honor to be called of God into the ministry of the church. How do you know if God is calling you?

First, there is an inward call. Through his Spirit, God speaks to those persons he has called to serve as pastors. The great Reformer, Martin Luther, described this inward call as "God's voice heard by faith." Those whom God has called know this call by a sense of leading, purpose, and growing commitment.

Charles Spurgeon identified the first sign of God's call to the ministry as "an intense, all-absorbing desire for the work." Those called by God sense a growing compulsion to preach and teach the Word, and to minister to the people of God. This sense of compulsion should prompt the believer to consider whether God may be calling him to the ministry. Has God gifted you with the fervent desire to preach? Has he equipped you with the gifts necessary for ministry? Do you love God's Word and feel called to teach? Spurgeon warned those who sought his counsel not to preach if they could help it. "But," Spurgeon continued, "if he cannot help it, and he must preach or die, then he is the man." That sense of urgent commission is one of the central marks of an authentic call.

Second, there is the external call. Baptists believe that God uses the congregation to "call out the called" to ministry. The congregation must evaluate and affirm the calling and gifts of the believer who feels so called. As a family of faith, the congregation should recognize and celebrate the gifts of ministry given to its members, and take responsibility to encourage those whom God has called to respond to that call with joy and submission.

These days, many persons think of careers rather than callings. The biblical challenge to "consider your call" should be extended from the call to salvation to the call to the ministry.

John Newton once remarked that "None but he who made the world can make a Minister of the Gospel." Only God can call a true minister, and only he can grant the minister the gifts necessary for service. But the great promise of Scripture is that God does call ministers, and presents these servants as gifts to the church.

One key issue here is a common misunderstanding about the will of God. As Paul makes clear in Romans 12:2, it is good, worthy of eager acceptance, and perfect. Those called by God to preach will be given a desire to preach as well as the gifts of preaching. Beyond this, the God-called preacher will feel the same compulsion as the great Apostle, who said, "Woe to me if I do not preach the gospel!" (1 Cor. 9:16, ESV).

Consider your calling. Do you sense that God is calling you to ministry, whether as pastor or another servant of the church? Do you burn with a compulsion to proclaim the Word, share the gospel, and care for God's flock? Has this call been confirmed and encouraged by those Christians who know you best?

In this new and important book, Brian Croft presents a bold and biblical understanding of the call to ministry. Along the way, Brian clarifies many issues of contemporary confusion, and his commitment to the local church ensures that his understanding of the call to ministry is never severed from the context of God's people.

Few books are more timely than this one, and I am thankful to Brian Croft for his faithful and careful consideration of the call to ministry.

R. Albert Mohler, Jr.
President, The Southern Baptist Theological Seminary

PREFACE

A great need emerged early in my pastorate. The church saw steady growth in the first few years, which included some new students from a local seminary. As I began to build relationships with these young men pursuing Christian ministry, I found many encouraging qualities among them all. They loved God. They had been transformed by the gospel. They loved the local church. They felt the call of God to pursue full-time occupational ministry. They all came to seminary with the expectation of being trained for the ministry.

However, a common cause of concern arose among these young men. Most of them had come to seminary to pursue Christian ministry without any kind of corporate affirmation from a local church. This seminary, like most, requires an affirmation from a local church for admission to the school. Yet, as I investigated more, the affirmation that most received consisted of mere approval to attend, rather than a corporate affirmation from a local church of the man's gifts for the ministry through a process of testing, watching, and praying.

I also found that most seminarians also expected that the seminary would take the responsibility of affirming and preparing them for the challenges and struggles of ministry. But as Albert Mohler, President of the Southern Baptist Theological Seminary, has stated on more than one occasion,

> I emphatically believe that the best and most proper place for the education and preparation of pastors is in the local church. We should be ashamed that churches fail miserably in their responsibility to train future pastors. Established pastors should be ashamed if they are not pouring themselves into the lives of young men whom God has called into the teaching and leadership ministry of the church.[1]

If the seminaries expect the local church to take the responsibility, and the local church presumes that the seminary will assume the reins, then who is truly responsible and ultimately accountable to God? And once that question is answered, how does the responsible party proceed with the task?

My aim for this book is to answer these essential questions and resolve this quandary that for decades has placed unnecessary pressure upon seminaries and Bible colleges, confused those seeking a pastoral calling for ministry, and allowed the local church to neglect that divine call which God has placed solely upon his particular assemblies. May the labor of this work contribute to an awakening of the local church to test, train, affirm, and send those who are truly called of God.

Brian Croft
Auburndale Baptist Church
Louisville, Kentucky
January 2010

INTRODUCTION

Arguably no work equals the assessment made by Charles Bridges (1794–1869) of the call of God on someone's life and the responsibility of those involved. In Bridges' book *The Christian Ministry*, he places the responsibility of determining a man's call into the ministry upon the conscience of the individual *and* upon the local church to which that man is committed. Bridges calls this evaluation process the internal and external call of God:

> The *external call* is a commission received from and recognized by the Church, not indeed qualifying the minister, but accrediting him, whom God had internally and suitably qualified. This call communicates therefore only official authority. The *internal call* is the voice and power of the Holy Spirit, directing the will and the judgment, and conveying personal qualifications. Both calls, however—though essentially distinct in their character and source—are indispensable for the exercise of our commission.[1]

Bridges states that, for an individual to know he is called of God to serve in the ministry, he must have received an *internal call*, which is the God-given desire within him to do the work of the ministry and his own conviction that he has been gifted and empowered by God's Spirit to do so.

This person must also possess an *external call*, which is the affirmation from the local church that this person possesses the gifts and godly character suitable for a Christian minister. Bridges, Charles Spurgeon, and many other godly men whom God used in the past to prepare those called into the ministry, all agree that both the internal and external calls are important for a person to possess in order to enter into the work of the ministry.

Unfortunately, this process is mostly lost today. In fact, it has practically vanished over the past century, which is why its recovery is needed even more. An argument for the necessity of both the internal and external calls into ministry is what you will find in the pages of this book.

This argument will be centered on God's design for his people in the Bible. It will identify who it is that God has placed as responsible for granting this external calling and for receiving it. Once a convincing argument has been made of the external call's importance, we will consider how a local church fulfills this role, and what is at stake if the church neglects it. Because of the kinds of questions that often come with this discussion, the chapter headings are styled as questions, thus highlighting the common probing that accompanies this issue.

The aim of this book is to challenge our visions and practices in order that we may think differently than before. God's calling for all of us as Christ's followers in the church ought to inspire us. May we therefore be encouraged by the great privilege God has given us as his kingdom-people in the church, both universal and local, of being on the front lines of his glorious, eternal, and kingdom-work on earth.

Prologue: To what is the pastor called?

IN THIS CHAPTER

God as Shepherd before the Fall →
Shepherding God's people—Israel →
Shepherding God's people—the church →
The Chief Shepherd eternally shepherding his people →

Chapter 1

Therefore, I exhort the elders among you, as your
fellow elder and witness of the sufferings of Christ,
and a partaker also of the glory that is to be
revealed, shepherd the flock of God among you ...
And when the Chief Shepherd appears, you will
receive the unfading crown of glory.

–1 Peter 5:1–2, 4

Before we explore questions about who receives the external
call to pastor, how that call happens, and who carries it out,
it seems appropriate to begin with some thoughts about God's
design for the care of his people, and how God calls his people
to execute that care in the lives of one another. God's purpose
and design in his care for his people are evident from the very
beginning of his interactions with the people he created, and
they run through the entire narrative of the Bible. The story line
of the Scriptures evidences God's design through the undeniable
presence of this important theme: It is God's design for God's
appointed leaders to instruct, care for, and shepherd God's
people under God's authority.

Though we see a theme of God as the Shepherd of his people
all through the Bible, some today think it is unhelpful to think
of God's care for his people in this way. A very famous and
influential senior pastor of one of the largest churches in America
was asked at the turn of the twenty-first century whether or
not we should stop speaking about pastors as "shepherds." He
emphatically stated,

> Absolutely. That word needs to go away. Jesus talked
> about shepherds because there was one over there in a
> pasture he could point to. But to bring in that imagery
> today and say, "Pastor, you're the shepherd of the flock,"
> no. I've never seen a flock. I've never spent five minutes

19

with a shepherd. It was culturally relevant in the time of Jesus, but it's not culturally relevant any more. Nothing works in our culture with that model except this sense of the gentle, pastoral care. Obviously that is a facet of church ministry, but that's not leadership.[1]

Is there merit in this critique? Is the image of God's care for his people as the Shepherd's care for his sheep unnecessary? Outdated? An unhelpful picture of leadership? On the contrary, the image seems to capture the essence of the role to which God has called pastors.

Creation

The Bible begins its historical narrative with a world that is foreign to us today.[2] God created the heavens, the earth, and all living creatures (Gen. 1–2). He also created man and woman in his image (1:27) and saw that all that he had made was very good (1:31). He placed the man and woman in the Garden of Eden, where they were to rule over his creation and be fruitful and multiply. The garden was beautiful, and in it there flowed a river to water the garden and a tree of life that was good for food (2:9–10). This world was perfectly made: man was created in the image of God, man enjoyed unhindered fellowship with God, and man ruled over the creation while fully submitting to God's rule over him.

As a result, man also enjoyed the unhindered care, leadership, and authority of God in his life. God perfectly led man, and man perfectly followed. Man trusted in God's goodness, care, and provision, and did not resent the authority that the Creator exercised over the creation.

Fall

Nevertheless, this world in Genesis 1–2 is not the world we live in today. The reality of life is that something is really wrong with the world and with those who were made in God's image.

This more familiar understanding of the world is traced back to Genesis 3, where Adam and Eve sinned by disobeying God's word when they ate from the tree of the knowledge of good and evil (3:6). God told them not to eat from this tree or they would die (2:17). Satan tempted Eve, and she ate from the tree and gave some of its fruit to her husband (3:6). Instead of obeying God's command, they rebelled against him. They wanted to rule, not to be ruled by God.

As a result of their sin, the curse of death of which God had warned them came upon them and all his creation. On that day, sin with all its ramifications entered the world. Adam and Eve were removed from the garden and the tree of life, whose fruit would grant eternal life (3:22). Pain and difficulty would now mar life, from childbirth to daily labor (3:16). A great separation from their once-unhindered fellowship with God now existed. Most significantly, death entered the world with sin and affected all creation, including man created in the image of God. As a result, man would suffer not only death, but also the effects of death, such as old age, pain, and suffering.

Another significant ramification of man being separated from God was that God no longer led, cared for, and shepherded man as he had done before. Man rebelled against God's authority instead of wholly submitting to it. Man rejected the care of his loving Creator; he strayed from the Good Shepherd. From this place in the story line of the Bible, the desperate need for redemption began. It is quickly revealed in the narrative that only a sovereign, eternal God could intervene to save creation from this curse. Therefore, the hope of the gospel, which included the promise of restored unhindered fellowship with the Chief Shepherd, began to unfold in a glorious work of redemption that culminated in Jesus's life, death, and resurrection.

The life of Israel
God determined to redeem mankind through a chosen nation

that would be his people among all the other nations of the earth. This nation was promised to Abraham (Gen. 12) through a child, Isaac, who would be born (Gen. 21). From Isaac came a son, Jacob, who would later be called Israel. It was through Jacob's twelve sons that the nation of Israel began. Through one of Jacob's sons, Joseph, the nation of Israel was established in Egypt, where they multiplied greatly (Exod. 1:7), yet they eventually became enslaved to the Egyptians. God, however, had promised hundreds of years before this (Gen. 15:13–14) that he would deliver them from their oppression and judge the nation which held them captive. Through the events of this deliverance, God would appoint a leader to lead, care for, and shepherd his people. That leader was Moses.

Like many whom God divinely appoints to lead and care for his people, Moses felt inadequately equipped for the task. In fact, during the burning bush experience, when God called Moses to deliver his people (Exod. 3:10), Moses tried several times to wiggle out of this calling. As Moses reminded God of his inability to execute this task (3:11; 4:1, 10), we see a pattern emerge for all those called to lead and care for God's people— God's empowerment to carry out the call. God gave Moses the power, words, and ability to be faithful to this call to lead and shepherd his people. It was God himself who led his people *through* the one appointed by him to do so. God told Moses to come before Pharaoh and the people of Israel in his name, the great I AM (Exod. 3:14). God gave him the power to perform signs and wonders in order to affirm that God was with him (4:1–5). It was God who even spoke for him (4:10–12). When God appoints one to lead, care for, and shepherd his people, he works through him to care for his people and accomplish his purposes.

Devastating consequences follow, however, when one who leads God's people fails to guide them faithfully. Through God's guidance and power, Moses delivered his people, led them to make a covenant with God, and journeyed up the mountain to retrieve God's law for them. While Moses was gone, Aaron failed to lead faithfully as a result of pressure from the people (32:1) and gross idolatry resulted (32:1–10). When the shepherd fails to lead, the sheep are easily led astray.

This theme continued as the monarchy of Israel was established. Israel were God's chosen people who were to be led by God, yet in the people's disobedience and lack of faith, they wanted a king to lead them like all the other nations (1 Sam. 8:5). Though this desire was a rejection of God's leadership (8:8), God allowed their pursuit of a king, but warned them of the disaster that awaited them. All that the Lord warned would take place (8:10–22) came to pass when Saul assumed the role of king over Israel. The reign of King Saul brought heartache, tragedy, disobedience to the Lord, and, ultimately the suffering of God's people. Yet God, in his mercy, selected a king for himself (16:1) who, despite his imperfections, would rule in righteousness, justice, and humility before the Lord. David, a shepherd himself, was God's king known best as a man after God's own heart (Acts 13:22). He was God's appointed shepherd to care for his people on God's behalf. Even more significantly, it was through David that the Messiah—God's eternal Redeemer, Shepherd and King—would come to redeem his people (2 Sam. 7).

This theme of God's righteous, expected shepherd developed further in Israel's history through the prophets and the time of Israel's exile. The prophets first accused Israel's leaders of being unfaithful and negligent shepherds of God's people. The prophets Jeremiah, Zechariah, and Ezekiel all extended warnings to these unfaithful shepherds about the ramifications of their neglect:

> "Woe to the shepherds who are destroying and scattering the sheep of My pasture!" declares the LORD. Therefore thus says the LORD God of Israel concerning

the shepherds who are tending My people: "You have scattered My flock and driven them away, and have not attended to them; behold, I am about to attend to you for the evil of your deeds," declares the LORD.

Jer. 23:1–2

The unfaithful shepherd not only harms the flock of God by his neglect, but also brings ultimate judgment upon himself because of it. Yet, in the midst of these devastating consequences of unfaithful shepherds leading God's people, God appointed a shepherd to faithfully lead, care for, and shepherd his people.

This appointed shepherd, who pointed to the Good Shepherd and Redeemer to come, was the prophet Zechariah. In the absence of faithful shepherds, God called Zechariah to assume this position of shepherd which led to his suffering as even he was rejected by his people: "'Awake, O sword, against My Shepherd, and against the man, My Associate,' declares the LORD of hosts, 'Strike the Shepherd that the sheep may be scattered'" (Zech. 13:7). Zechariah's suffering pointed to the Good Shepherd who would suffer to redeem his people. The word of the prophets concluded that God's people were scattered, disobedient, and discouraged, yet also encouraged them to wait for the hope of the promised Redeemer and Good Shepherd (Ezek. 34:23). Despite this tragic history of God's people, God was faithful to the covenant he made with his people to send a Redeemer and usher in the long-awaited kingdom of God.

The life of Christ

After many years of silence, God broke through the despair and suffering with a voice of one crying out in the wilderness to make ready the way of the Lord (Mark 1:3). This voice was John the Baptist, who was the forerunner to prepare others for the coming of the Redeemer. All four Gospels identify Jesus as this Redeemer, the long-awaited Messiah who was to save his people from their sins and usher in the kingdom of God. Mark points us to Jesus Christ, the Redeemer, in Jesus's first recorded words of his Gospel account: "The time is fulfilled, and the kingdom of God is at hand; repent and believe in the gospel" (Mark 1:15). The kingdom had come in Jesus.

Jesus came in the authority of God as the Son of God (Mark 1:1), as evidenced by his power over sickness, demons, and death. However, Jesus also displayed his authority as ruler over God's kingdom, as he claimed to be the one who was to come and faithfully rule, lead, care for, and shepherd his people. John affirmed this claim as he recorded these words from Jesus: "I am the good shepherd; and I know My own, and My own know Me, even as the Father knows Me and I know the Father; and I lay down My life for the sheep" (John 10:14–15).

Jesus proved to be this Good Shepherd who would lay down his life for his sheep, fulfilling the words of Zechariah. Mark's first recorded words of Jesus following Jesus's last Passover meal with his disciples are those same words of Zechariah: "You will all fall away, because it is written, 'I will strike down the shepherd and the sheep shall be scattered'" (Mark 14:27). Zechariah spoke those words as an indictment of the unfaithful shepherds of Israel, but Jesus used them to refer to his perfect faithfulness in laying down his life for his sheep, though they too would scatter for a time until he was reunited with them after his resurrection (Mark 14:28).

Following his resurrection, Jesus spoke of the authority that is now eternally his in God's kingdom: "All authority has been given to Me in heaven and on earth. Go therefore and make disciples of all the nations, baptizing them in the name of the Father and the Son and the Holy Spirit, teaching them to observe all that I commanded you; and lo, I am with you always, even to the end of the age" (Matt. 28:18–20). As the Good Shepherd, and in his authority given from God, Jesus now commanded his disciples to go and gather his sheep from all the nations.

The life of the church

Jesus died, rose from the dead, appeared to many witnesses, and ascended to be with the Father. As he ascended, he also empowered his disciples by the Holy Spirit to be the ones to lead, care for, and shepherd God's people. The church was birthed at Pentecost (Acts 2), and the apostles went out to be Christ's witnesses to the world (1:8). As the early church was built, so was the leadership structure by which the Good Shepherd would care for his sheep.

The apostles were the first to be appointed by God to lead and shepherd his people under Christ's authority. This transfer of authority is evidenced in Jesus's conversation with Peter, as recorded by John, in which Jesus asked Peter three times if he loved him. Peter said, "Yes, Lord; You know that I love You." In light of Peter's answers, Jesus responded all three times by saying, "Shepherd My sheep" (John 21:15–17). This same apostolic authority was also given to Paul as he was radically converted when Christ appeared to him on the Damascus road (Acts 9:3–6) and was appointed apostle to the Gentiles (9:15–16). Through these apostles, the early church was established and the responsibility to lead, care for, and shepherd God's people under God's authority passed to pastors.

The earliest picture of this model is found in the book of Acts where this responsibility was divided among those who would serve tables (6:2) and those devoted to prayer and the ministry of the Word (6:4). The apostle Paul further developed this idea when he wrote to Timothy and described the qualifications of the biblical office which would lead, care for, and shepherd God's people within the local church—that of the pastor (1 Tim. 3:1–7).[3] Paul further wrote to Titus to appoint elders (pastors) in every city (Titus 1:5). The pastor was now the one appointed by God and empowered by the Holy Spirit to shepherd Christ's sheep, as described by Peter:

Therefore, I exhort the elders among you, as your fellow elder and witness of the sufferings of Christ, and a partaker also of the glory that is to be revealed, shepherd the flock of God among you, exercising oversight not under compulsion, but voluntarily, according to the will of God; and not for sordid gain, but with eagerness; nor yet as lording it over those allotted to your charge, but proving to be examples to the flock. And when the Chief Shepherd appears, you will receive the unfading crown of glory.

1 Peter 5:1–4

Here we can observe the number of shepherds appointed (plural), the manner in which they should shepherd (voluntarily, eagerly, and exemplarily), and the one to whom these shepherds of God's people would be accountable—the Chief Shepherd, Jesus Christ. Hence God's appointed leadership structure for his people was established until the Chief Shepherd returns for his church and consummates his kingdom.

New creation

The unfolding of God's redemptive plan for all creation will come to an end. The final destination for those who follow Christ is not a disembodied existence of life after death. When Jesus returns, he will come for his bride, judge the nations, punish the wicked, and fully consummate his kingdom in the new heaven and new earth. This state is known as the new creation, where the curse of sin will be fully and permanently reversed. There God's kingdom people will experience not just a physical resurrection, but also eternal fellowship with Jesus our Savior, King, and Shepherd.

In this new creation, God's design for his people is not simply fellowship with Jesus. Rather he will restore his role as the Good Shepherd to his people through Jesus, the one appointed by God to be their Shepherd. John gives us a powerful picture of this restored relationship with the Chief Shepherd and of his redeemed sheep ruling with him:

> Then one of the elders answered, saying to me, "These who are clothed in the white robes, who are they, and where have they come from?" I said to him, "My lord, you know." And he said to me, "These are the ones who come out of the great tribulation, and they have washed their robes and made them white in the blood of the Lamb. For this reason, they are before the throne of God; and they serve Him day and night in His temple; and He who sits on the throne will spread His tabernacle over them. They will hunger no longer, nor thirst anymore; nor will the sun beat down on them, nor any heat; for the Lamb in the center of the throne will be their shepherd, and will guide them to springs of the water of life; and God will wipe every tear from their eyes."

Rev. 7:13–17

Christ, who came as the Lamb of God to be slaughtered on behalf of his people, will now be the eternal Shepherd to his people. Even those who are appointed for a time by God to shepherd the flock of God in the local church will receive their reward by being led, cared for, and shepherded forever by the Good Shepherd who laid down his life for his sheep. For these reasons, the imagery of a shepherd caring for his sheep is not unnecessary or outdated, but essential to understanding the shepherd's role now in the local church and how we will relate to Christ as his people in his consummated kingdom.

Understanding this unfolding story line of the Bible is indispensable for grasping God's design and plan for his creation and comprehending God's eternal purpose for how his people are to be led, cared for, and shepherded in a fallen world as we await Christ's return. As we see this biblical foundation for the role of the pastor in the local church, how, then, are these appointed shepherds from God to be recognized, affirmed, and placed in a position to shepherd God's people? We now turn to this question, which will be discussed throughout the remainder of the book.

Who is responsible for the external call?

IN THIS CHAPTER

Who is not responsible →
Who is responsible →
Uniting around our responsibility →

I emphatically believe that the best and most proper place for the education and preparation of pastors is in the local church.

—R. Albert Mohler, Jr.

A variety of opinions exists regarding who is responsible for granting an external call. Potentially responsible parties include seminaries, Bible colleges, mission organizations, para-church ministries, Christian friends, and denominational leaders. Much as a timid man refuses to accept the blame for a bad decision, so the responsibility for training and affirming an individual's calling into the ministry too often gets passively handed over to others. In light of this confusion, identifying who is *not* responsible for this task will clarify who *is* truly responsible.

Unmerited responsibility

For over a century, the predominant default answer to this question has been seminaries and Bible colleges. These organizations have been likely candidates because some of the most brilliant scholars in theology, church history, hermeneutics, and the original biblical languages can be found at many of the best-known seminaries and Bible colleges in the world. There are gifted pastors on the faculty with decades of pastoral experience that is brought to the classroom. These academic settings require a rigorous standard of reading, studying, and theological engagement that few have the personal discipline to achieve on their own. Yet, as important a role as theological education can play in the preparation of the called of God, God has not ultimately commissioned these institutions to fulfill this responsibility.

Mission organizations have also often been the bearers of this burden. Many of the pioneering missionary efforts in the last 200 years began because few churches and denominations would support the sending of missionaries to very dangerous places.

The great Scottish Presbyterian missionary John Paton took the gospel to the New Hebrides islands in the mid-nineteenth century with little support from churches and fellow Christians. Paton recalls an older Christian even trying to discourage him from fulfilling this call to the heathen lands by warning him, "You will be eaten by cannibals!"[1]

As a result of this lack of support, the missionary zeal of the eighteenth and nineteenth centuries caused several missionary sending organizations to emerge, and God has greatly used them to take the gospel to the nations. Because of the missionary forces of the International Mission Board, the China Inland Mission, the Voice of the Martyrs, To Every Tribe Missions, and many others, it can be difficult to imagine that God has created a different design for the sending of missionaries into the lost world—but the Bible does reveal a different structure.

Para-church and denominational ministries, though less likely candidates for this task, have nevertheless been entrusted by some for their training and affirmation for gospel ministry. In the eyes of many in the younger generation, these ministries have even assumed the complete role of filling the void of the local church. If you doubt the validity of that statement, just spend a little time on a typical college campus and wander along to the evening gathering of one of the various campus ministries represented. There you will find professing Christians, faithful attendees, and even those sensing a call into the ministry, who have no further Christian affiliation, nor feel any need for one, apart from that evening gathering. In addition, many of these ministries' staff positions are filled through those trained solely within the organizations. Though there continue to be professing Christians and those feeling an internal call into the ministry who see these kinds of ministries as their outlet for training and affirmation, it does not change the reality that God has appointed a different strategy for the testing, training, affirming, and sending of those he calls.

Individual Christians who know a person well can also wrongfully assume this role. These are Christians who are spread all over the map and who have been a significant influence upon the individual throughout his life. They knew him when he was a boy. They knew him before he was a Christian. They once taught his Bible study class. They were praying with him when he surrendered his life to God to pursue the ministry. Surely, of all the potentially responsible parties, these people are more equipped to assess the call, character, and qualifications of the individual? Yet, as helpful as these credible witnesses are to guide this brother in pursuing the call of God, God has prescribed a different solution.

Unquestionably, God has mightily used seminaries, mission organizations, para-church ministries, and individual Christians in men's upbringing to equip the called and build God's kingdom powerfully throughout the centuries. There is no debate about their role and impact in furthering the gospel and making disciples in the past, present, or future. The problem, however, is that none of these options has been biblically commissioned by God to take the full and ultimate responsibility for testing, training, affirming, and sending those who are called to be pastors and missionaries. So, then, who is ultimately responsible?

The local church

It is the local church that God has appointed to be the agent to test, train, affirm, and send those who are called. Because of this truth, the local church must embrace this enormous responsibility. This call has been the responsibility of the church from the beginning, as we see the church in Antioch (Acts 13) embrace it. This church is a great example in helping the local church better understand its role in the external call in our day. Luke tells of Saul and Barnabas preparing to be sent on their first missionary journey. Here is the scene as the church sends them:

> Now there were at Antioch, in the church that was there, prophets and teachers: Barnabas, and Simeon who was called Niger, and Lucius of Cyrene, and Manaen who had been brought up with Herod the tetrarch, and Saul. While they were ministering to the Lord and fasting, the Holy Spirit said, "Set apart for Me Barnabas and Saul for the work to which I have called them." Then, when they had fasted and prayed and laid their hands on them, they sent them away.
>
> Acts 13:1–3

The responsibility of the external call is centered on the local church, as evidenced in the sole presence of the church at Antioch. James Montgomery Boice makes a similar point and speaks of the church of Antioch in this way: "God does what he does through tools, and in the case of missionary work the tool God uses is his church. At Antioch we have an example of a mighty mission tool, a church that was established, well-taught, integrated, active, and seeking God's direction."[2]

The prophets and teachers (v. 1) were the early church pastors and leaders. The central means by which God revealed his will for Saul and Barnabas were the other pastors and believers of the church in Antioch. In the calling of Saul and Barnabas, we observe where this responsibility was centralized as well as who was given the role in this process to affirm and send ministers.

Paul and Barnabas were first recognized by the pastors. These leaders were engaging in their normal routine, as Luke reveals that they were ministering to the Lord and fasting (v. 2). In other words, they were doing the work of the church by preaching and teaching God's Word, shepherding the church, and being deliberately prayerful about it. Fasting is the purposeful setting aside of eating to concentrate on spiritual issues, predominantly through prayer. In the faithfulness of these leaders, the Holy Spirit revealed God's will for Saul and Barnabas. They were to be "Set apart ... for the work to which [God had] called them" (v. 2).

Consider for a moment the guidance of God in this decision. First and foremost, they certainly had the message of the Holy Spirit (v. 2). But they were also aware of the fruitfulness of Saul and Barnabas's previous labor. At the end of Acts 11, Saul and Barnabas came to the church at Antioch, where they fellowshipped for an entire year (11:26), met with the church, and cared for them. The church and its leaders had the evidence of God's call on these men's lives because of the fruitfulness of their past labor *among them*. They were therefore able to affirm them, not only by God's present guidance by his Spirit, but also by these men's past fruitful labors, all in the wisdom of God through their continual fasting and praying. Then, at the appropriate time, the leaders laid their hands on Saul and Barnabas to affirm them in this call (13:3); this was the affirmation not simply of the leaders, but also of the entire church (see Acts 6:5–6 and 14:27).

Lastly, Saul and Barnabas were affirmed by the local church. Since the Antioch church and its leaders had been able to watch their lives, see their fruitful ministry within this particular church, and seek the Lord's guidance, they now officially applied the external call of God to Saul and Barnabas as they laid their hands on them in affirmation (on behalf of the church; v. 3). Then "they sent them away" (v. 3). The Spirit also worked through the church; the church sent them (v. 3), but Luke reveals that the Spirit also sent them (v. 4). The church's involvement in their ministry didn't stop at their sending, for as Saul and Barnabas returned from their efforts they "gathered the church together [and] began to report all things that God had done with them" (Acts 14:27).

The leaders (prophets/teachers) and the church by the Holy Spirit played a central role in giving the external call to Saul and Barnabas for them to do the work to which God had called them. How do we measure the importance of this affirmation from the church in Antioch? It resulted in God continuing to build his church as Jews and Gentiles throughout the Roman world heard the gospel.

Although this picture in Acts focuses on the affirming and sending of missionaries, supporting texts throughout the New Testament should cause us to conclude that this same process applies for all those called into the gospel ministry. Paul wrote to Titus, instructing him to "appoint elders in every city" (Titus 1:5). Paul exhorted Timothy, "The things which you have heard from me in the presence of many witnesses, entrust these to faithful men who will be able to teach others also" (2 Tim. 2:2). This picture in Acts can also be seen in Timothy's pastoral calling, as Paul refers to other pastors having laid hands on Timothy in affirmation of his gifts and calling (1 Tim. 4:14). Regardless of the type of gospel ministry, God has designed all pastors and missionaries to be identified by pastors and affirmed by the local church.

A convenient ambiguity

Although there are many clear observations to make from these opening verses of Acts 13, a convenient ambiguity exists regarding the detailed outworking of this process. In other words, the description of the process is clear, yet the prescription of the process can be applied faithfully in a variety of contexts. The clarity of the passage should therefore unite local churches in this common call, even though we may differ in our structure of polity.

For example, an elder-led congregational church, an elder-ruled church, a single pastor–staff-led church, and even a deacon-led church can all read Acts 13:1–3 and develop their own outworkings of this process of testing, training, affirming, and sending within their particular contexts and structures of polity. This account in Acts clearly shows us that the local church was the primary instrument used, that the leaders of the church led in this process, and that the congregation was involved to some degree in these men's lives to affirm and send them. Where the balance of authority lands and how roles are distributed within the local church depends on the structure of the church. Although I have a particular conviction regarding which structure of polity is most biblical, nevertheless, this ambiguity exists. Thus, it allows us to disagree on polity and yet lock arms, realizing that our local churches are still ultimately responsible.

The detailed process is unclear, yet it is clear where the responsibility falls. God has called out a people for salvation from every tribe, tongue, people, and nation to build his kingdom and to display his glory to the nations. Although God uses many people and organizations to accomplish many purposes, the authority and responsibility given by God for building his kingdom and displaying his glory rest solely upon his redeemed people within the context of the local church. God has divinely ordained the local church to grant the external call to an individual seeking the call of God. May our individual local churches and our leaders within be awakened to feel the weight of this responsibility so that they will take hold of it and hold it fast to the end.

Who should receive the external call?

IN THIS CHAPTER

A Christian man who desires this work ➔

A Christian man who qualifies biblically ➔

A Christian man who loves the local church ➔

It need scarcely be said that piety is essential. No amount of talent, no extent of education, no apparent brilliancy of fervor, should even be allowed to gain admission into the ministry for one whose piety there is a reason to doubt, or who has not a more than ordinary active and consistent holiness.

–Basil Manly, Jr.

Who should receive the external call? It is essential that a church think through this question biblically before it acts to confer its blessing on any man pursuing ministry. Sadly, many churches today base their "external call" on nothing more than a man's sense of *internal* "calling"—his own subjective perception of his desire to do the work of the ministry and of his giftedness for that work. To be sure, a man's own assessment of his desire and giftedness for the work of the ministry does play a key role in determining whether a church should grant that man the external call. Nonetheless, churches have a responsibility to base their external call not, primarily, on a mystical, subjective, and unfalsifiable feeling in the man himself, but rather on a tangible process that tests a man's qualifications for ministry against those laid out in Scripture.

The aim of this chapter is to consider what the Bible reveals about assessing who is to receive this external call from the local church and how pastors and theologians throughout church history have evaluated men who believed they were sensing an internal calling from God. Regarding the question, "What kind of man receives an external call from a local church?" saints from the past and present have offered four answers in light of the biblical qualifications for pastors found in 1 Timothy 3:1–7.[1]

A Christian man transformed by the gospel of Jesus Christ

Any man who would dare enter the sacred office of minister of the gospel must first be transformed by the gospel. The gospel is the message of salvation from sin and God's wrath that a sinner receives by grace through repentance of sin and faith in the person and work of Jesus Christ. Many would attest to this being a fairly obvious answer to the question and somewhat of an oxymoron to think that a man would enter the ministry without saving faith in Christ. It must, however, have been a legitimate concern in the seventeenth century, otherwise Richard Baxter would not have begun his celebrated book, *The Reformed Pastor*, in this way:

> Take heed to yourselves, lest you be void of that saving grace of God which you offer to others, and be strangers to the effectual working of that gospel which you preach; and lest, while you proclaim to the world the necessity of a Saviour, your own hearts should neglect him and you should miss of an interest in him and his saving benefits. Take heed to yourselves, lest you perish, while you call upon others to take heed of perishing; and lest you famish yourselves while you prepare food for them ... Many have warned others that they come not to that place of torment, while yet they hastened to it themselves; many a preacher is now in hell, who hath a hundred times called upon his hearers to use the utmost care and diligence to escape it.[2]

Baxter's warning should resonate with those who love Christ and his church just as much in the twenty-first century. Much is at stake if local churches neglect to evaluate and warn a man who is still in darkness, enslaved to sin, in complete rebellion against God, and yet placed in a position of being entrusted with the gospel and shepherding redeemed souls while his own soul perishes.

A Christian man who desires this fine work

The apostle Paul instructs his young protégé in the faith, writing, "It is a trustworthy statement: if any man aspires to the office of overseer [pastor], it is a fine work he desires to do" (1 Tim. 3:1). The great nineteenth-century Baptist Charles Spurgeon lectured young men preparing for the ministry in this way: "The first sign of the heavenly calling is an intense, all-absorbing desire for the work."[3] There must be a strong, unquenchable desire to do the work of a pastor—a desire to preach God's Word, shepherd God's people, evangelize the lost, disciple the spiritually immature, and serve the local church.

Spurgeon confirms that this aspiration, which comes from above, can be known through a desire to do nothing else:

> If any student in this room could be content to be a newspaper editor, or a grocer, or a farmer, or a doctor, or a lawyer, or a senator, or a king, in the name of heaven and earth, let him go his way; he is not the man in whom dwells the Spirit of God in its fullness, for a man so filled with God would utterly weary of any pursuit but that for which his inmost soul pants. If on the other hand, you can say that for all the wealth of both the Indies you could not and dare not espouse any other calling so as to be put aside from preaching the gospel of Jesus Christ, then depend upon it, if other things be equally satisfactory, you have the signs of this apostleship. We must feel that woe is unto us if we preach not the gospel; the word of God must be unto us as fire in our bones, otherwise, if we undertake the ministry, we shall be unhappy in it, shall be unable to bear the self-denials incident to it, and shall be of little service to those among whom we minister.[4]

Paul writes that the man who desires to do this divine work is pursuing a fine work. Nevertheless, an unquenchable longing for this work is required, for it is a work fraught with struggles, challenges, discouragements, pressures, and spiritual battles that can cripple the strongest of men whose desire for this labor is ordinary. It must be a desire that cannot be stolen when your brother betrays you; that cannot be weakened when your job is threatened; that cannot be quenched when physical, mental, and emotional fatigue firmly take root. This desire must so define the individual that the reality of an internal calling is unmistakable. Basil Manly, Jr., captures, not just the desire of the internal calling, but also how that desire should increase over time:

> This steadfast and divinely implanted desire to labor for souls is substantially what is meant by "the internal call." It may be distinguished from the early zeal, which young converts usually have, and which generally subsides into a calm principle of benevolent activity in their own particular sphere. In the man truly called, it grows, it increases. As he reflects on it, and prays about it, the great salvation becomes greater and nearer to him than when he first believed; the guilt and ruin of immortal souls weigh heavily upon him; he feels impelled to warn them to flee the wrath to come. Sometimes the thought presses on one, so that he cannot rest. The strongest promptings of self-interest, the greatest timidity and natural reserve, the most violent opposition of irreligious relatives and influential friends, and even the most serious peril, prove insufficient to check this holy ardor. The man is made to feel that for him all other avocations are trifling, all worldly employments unattractive. "Woe is unto me," he cries, "if I preach not the gospel!" Jails, and fetters, and the stake, have no terrors for him comparable with the guilt of disobeying Jesus, and the frown of his redeemer.[5]

Only a Christian man who possesses this kind of "irresistible, overwhelming craving and raging thirst"[6] for this fine work should receive the external call.

A Christian man whose character and life qualify him biblically

Many faithful, godly men throughout the ages, who displayed Christ in their characters and modeled sacrificial service to his church, were not called to the work of pastor/elder. Paul gives Timothy a list of qualifications for the office of pastor/elder that is separate from all other lists, including that for deacons (1 Tim. 3:8–13). This list demonstrates the unique calling and work that a pastor is set apart to do, and it also provides a way for others to evaluate externally and objectively a man claiming to possess the desire for this work. Paul's list of qualifications for the office of pastor can be summarized into five categories:

ABILITY TO TEACH

This is the primary qualification that sets apart the work of a pastor from all other forms of service in the church. Paul writes that this man must be "able to teach" (1 Tim. 3:2). This qualification refers not just to a man's desire to teach, but rather to the skill and ability to teach God's Word faithfully, accurately, and effectively. The reason for this qualification is given by Paul elsewhere, when he exhorts these uniquely called and gifted men to "Guard, through the Holy Spirit who dwells in us, the treasure" of the gospel (2 Tim. 1:14).

This requirement is also in place because of the warning of "stricter judgment" for those who teach in the church (James 3:1). Yet, for those who have been gifted by God for this task, they are to fulfill it humbly, clearly, passionately, and faithfully. The call is to preach the Word (2 Tim. 4:2) whatever the cost, seize every opportunity to make the gospel clear, present the treasure and value of Christ before hearers, call them to repent and believe, and then trust in the power of the Holy Spirit to perform the transforming work of the gospel. This ability to instruct God's people in his Word by "reprov[ing], rebuk[ing], exhort[ing]" (2 Tim. 4:2) is to define every man's gospel ministry, both public and private. As Roger Ellsworth has rightly observed, "Fail here and you would have failed in your central task."[7]

BLAMELESS REPUTATION

Paul's command that the pastor "must be above reproach" (1 Tim. 3:2) is listed to emphasize that the man should flee not just from evil, but from even the appearance of evil. For example, it is very hard to accuse a pastor of having an affair if everyone knows that he will never be alone in a room with any woman except his wife. This qualification is calling the pastor to live above any accusations that might be thrown his way by his consistent godly life and reputation among all people. Not being in bondage to any substance, but being self-controlled, affirms this reputation, which seems to be why Paul also lists "not addicted to wine" (v. 3).

This blameless reputation also includes having a "good reputation with those outside the church, so that he will not fall into reproach and the snare of the devil" (v. 7). This description is by no means an instruction to appease the world, but rather that the lost may "on account of [a pastor's] good deeds, as they observe them, glorify God in the day of visitation" (1 Peter 2:12).

FAITHFUL MANAGEMENT OF HIS FAMILY

This qualification is that a pastor be "the husband of one wife" (1 Tim. 3:2). This phrase is commonly misunderstood as meaning that a pastor must be married and cannot be single, but the qualification is not concerned with his marital status. It does demand, however, that a pastor be faithful to his one wife. The pastor's leadership in the home in regard to his wife is to be seen by his loving her deeply and sacrificially, "just as Christ also loved the church and gave Himself up for her" (Eph. 5:25). As this command is for all Christian men to love their wives in this way, the pastor is called to model it for his people.

This characteristic, joined with Paul's additional instruction to Timothy, also reveals that a woman is not to exercise authority over a man (1 Tim. 2:12). Just as men are to lead their families, God's design is for them also to lead the church.

The principle also applies to children in the home. The pastor is to shepherd, teach, care, and manage his children faithfully (1 Tim. 3:4). This admonition does not entail that he must have children or that his children must be converted; it is a qualification that any children must respect their father's authority as the God-appointed head and leader of the family. Paul gives a very profound reason: "if a man does not know how to manage his own household, how will he take care of the church of God?" (v. 5).

Another characteristic that greatly affects the whole family is being "hospitable" (1 Tim. 3:2). Most people connect this characteristic with welcoming people into their homes, which is correct, but it also implies welcoming and loving strangers. Most people are hospitable to the people they know and love, but few of us are hospitable to strangers we don't know. Paul requires that a pastor model this kind of sacrifice and willingness to care for others.

GODLY CHARACTER

Most of the characteristics Paul lists could be lumped into this category of godly character. The pastor is to be "temperate, prudent, respectable" (1 Tim. 3:2), as well as "gentle, peaceable" (v. 3). All these speak of the inward transformation of the gospel reflected in kindness, compassion, self-control with words and actions, and being honorable, humble, and full of discernment and wisdom. Too much emphasis cannot be placed on this requirement, as Basil Manly, Jr., observes:

It need scarcely be said that piety is essential. No amount of talent, no extent of education, no apparent brilliancy of fervor, should even be allowed to gain admission into the ministry for one whose piety there is a reason to doubt, or who has not a more than ordinary active and consistent holiness. A Christless minister is as horribly out of place as a ghastly skeleton in the pulpit bearing a torch in his hand.[8]

Ministers must not merely possess these godly characteristics, but they must also daily grow in them, as David Dickson writes: "Though the work of the eldership is in itself very honorable and very interesting, yet it will be dull, formal, and worthless unless there is a real and growing love to Jesus in our hearts. That is the only oil that will make the lamp burn and keep it burning."[9]

It is not an accident that most of Paul's qualifications fall into this category. For this reason, those who desire this work should labor diligently to grow in these qualities, knowing that it is the grace of God and the transforming power of the gospel that empowers the growth.

SPIRITUAL MATURITY

Many of these qualities also point to the requirement of spiritual maturity, but there are two qualities that specifically evidence this. First, the pastor is to be "free from the love of money" (1 Tim. 3:3). His primary responsibility is to preach and teach the Word of God and sacrificially care for his people. It would be a contradiction if the pastor's idol was money. The assessment of this qualification is not according to how much money a pastor has or will get paid, but to what he does with the money he has. Having a love for money has nothing to do with how much we have, but with our desire to have more and more of it. The desire for the fine work of gospel ministry will always work against a desire for personal material gain.

46

Second, as the spiritual leaders and doctrinal gatekeepers of the church, the pastors cannot be "new convert[s]" (1 Tim. 3:6), which implies that a spiritually immature man should not enter this work. This makes sense for several obvious reasons, but Paul in this text gives a specific one—"so that he will not become conceited and fall into the condemnation incurred by the devil" (v. 6). The office of pastor is one of importance, and an immature believer could get caught up in the power of the position instead of seeing this office as sacrifice and service to God and his people. Pursuing this office also places a man on the front line of spiritual attack from the enemy, which seems to be one of the several reasons why the New Testament calls for a plurality of godly, spiritually mature pastors/elders in a local church for accountability, fellowship, and accumulated wisdom (Titus 1:5; Acts 20:28; 1 Peter 5:1).

A Christian man who is intimately involved with the local church

No one wants a physician who may have finished medical school but has no understanding or knowledge of a hospital and the hands-on experience of treating sick people. Likewise, no one wants a pastor who is not involved and knowledgeable in the very setting in which he feels called to labor—the local church. Nor can a local church affirm someone who has not demonstrated to it the "desire and character" required for this office through his involvement with that church. Hence, for a local church to be able and equipped to give an external call to a man, that man must exhibit his internal calling within that church.

A Christian man's internal calling is demonstrated through his love and commitment to a local church. How sad, and all-too-common, it is for a young man to spend years in seminary and be cut off from any local-church involvement! Then he graduates and somehow thinks that a love for the local church will magically come with the salary he accepts from his first pastorate. Yet a love for the local church is displayed by a commitment to it, realizing that it is the means through which God primarily is building his kingdom and accomplishing his purposes in the world.

A Christian man's internal calling is also revealed to the members of a local congregation as his gifts are exercised within the body for all to observe. In considering the lists Paul gives us in Scripture, we see that there are many gifts a man called to this fine work should possess and use to serve that local church to which he has committed himself. Gifts to preach and teach publicly and privately, kindly care for the widows, be hospitable in his home, and share the gospel with unbelievers: all are gifts that Scripture tells us the pastor should possess.

As those gifts are used, the man's internal calling will bear fruit and will impact the lives of the people in that local church. God will use a man who is able to teach to sow fruitful seeds of the Word into people's hearts. God will use to impact lives a man who is willing to shower kindness and gentleness on an elderly lady sick in the hospital. God will use to impact lives a man who gives his money to help a family in need in the church, or who invites a lonely single individual after church to his home for the afternoon. As this man impacts others in the local church through deliberate and intimate involvement, God in his grace will equip the local church to affirm the internal calling of that brother with an external call.

Through reading Scripture and the lives of our heroes from church history, there are more than enough ways for a Christian man to identify an internal calling from God to pursue this fine work of gospel ministry. Yet these tools also reveal much that the local church can evaluate in a man through his service and fruitfulness among them. It is a Christian man—one who zealously desires this work, is able to teach, cares faithfully for his family, and exudes a godly, blameless, and spiritually mature character that is observed by others as he serves in the local church—who is to receive an external call. But what kind of local church gives this external call to one who desires to receive it? It is to this issue we now turn.

Who gives the external call?

IN THIS CHAPTER

A local church faithful to Scripture →
A local church with faithful shepherds →
A local church with faithful members →
A local church faithful in discipline →

Chapter 4

Every man who believes alone, that he is called of
God to the ministry, has reason to apprehend that
he is under delusion.

–J. L. Dagg

We are our least accurate critics. We either think too highly
of ourselves in personal evaluation, or we beat ourselves
up unnecessarily. For example, the preacher can rarely evaluate
his own sermons well. Preachers who think they delivered a
"home run" sermon are often humbled by a mediocre response
from their hearers. Likewise, a preacher often feels sorry for
himself after a perceived weak sermon, only to find that God
used it to bear much spiritual fruit. Certainly, God's grace and
power use weak and human vessels to accomplish his purposes.
These examples also reveal the need for every Christian man to
have other Christians in his life to aid him in self-evaluation.

Evaluating those called to the gospel ministry is no different.
This is why J. L. Dagg spoke so powerfully about the need for
an external call: "Every man who believes alone, that he is called
of God to the ministry, has reason to apprehend that he is under
delusion. If he finds that those who give proof that they honor
God and love the souls of men, do not discover his ministerial
qualifications, he has reason to suspect that they do not exist."[1]
Because we are often unable to evaluate ourselves objectively,
God places brothers and sisters from our local church in our
lives to play this role.

Thus far, I have argued that it is the responsibility of the local
church to test, train, affirm, and send those pursuing gospel
ministry. Yet Christians who have never witnessed a local
church engaging in this task may wonder, What kind of church
assumes this responsibility? Marks that identify a true church
of Jesus Christ do not necessarily include the assumption of
the responsibility of the external call.[2] Nevertheless, a local

church that assumes this responsibility is a faithful one, as Samuel Miller, who taught at Princeton Theological Seminary in the nineteenth century, observed: "No church, therefore, which neglects the proper education of her ministers, can be considered as faithful, either to her own most vital interests, or to the honour of her divine Head and Lord."[3]

Therefore, to answer the question "What kind of local church gives this affirmation?" we must consider other marks of a faithful and healthy church. There is no perfect church, but in a local church striving to function the way God desires, fertile ground exists for the seeds of faithfulness and health to take root and grow. Four areas of faithfulness are essential for a local church to grow in if it desires to be effective in giving an external call: centrality of Scripture, faithful shepherding, regenerate church membership, and church discipline.

A local church whose central focus and practice are determined by Scripture

In a time when entertainment and pragmatism drive much of the evangelical church, only a local church whose unshakable foundation for its faith and practice is God's Word will be equipped to test, train, affirm, and send. Obedience to Christ's commands presupposes a knowledge of these commands. Similarly, only through a commitment to Scripture can we know the imperatives that accompany an external call and how to apply them.

The first area to evaluate and identify is how we preach and teach God's Word. Expositional preaching is the most effective way to centralize God's Word in a sermon and service. Mark Dever, in his book *Nine Marks of a Healthy Church*, says, "Expositional preaching is that preaching which takes for the point of a sermon the point of a particular passage of Scripture."[4] This is best accomplished through the regular systematic preaching of individual books of the Bible. This

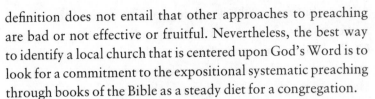
definition does not entail that other approaches to preaching are bad or not effective or fruitful. Nevertheless, the best way to identify a local church that is centered upon God's Word is to look for a commitment to the expositional systematic preaching through books of the Bible as a steady diet for a congregation.

In addition, biblical theology should be a regular part of the instruction of a church that is committed to Scripture. Teaching biblical theology refers to teaching the broader story line of the Bible with God's redemptive purposes in Christ in view, which ultimately helps us read, study, and understand the Bible more clearly. Without the proper instruction of God's Word in the church, not only will those called into ministry be confused and the church lost in its responsibility in the external call, but spiritual life will also be lacking in the church.

The second area in which to recognize this commitment is in the polity or structure of the church. Though structures vary from church to church, Scripture gives a template that is undeniably clear. The New Testament speaks of pastors/elders (1 Tim. 3:1–7) who are entrusted with preaching and teaching God's Word and shepherding God's people (1 Peter 5:1–4). Deacons (1 Tim. 3:8–13) serve in particular and practical ministries of the church. The congregation also plays a role within the biblical structure of the church, as seen most clearly in passages dealing with church discipline (Matt. 18:15–17; 1 Cor. 5:1–11). Yet the structure itself is not enough. Those who serve in these roles must also submit to biblical qualifications and applications. This biblical structure provides the proper authority over and oversight of those pursuing a call into the ministry, it models the calling they pursue, and it creates the process through which they seek to be affirmed.

The third area that reveals this commitment to Scripture is the kind of ministry in which the local church engages. The question does not pertain to whether a church is doing discipleship, evangelism, mercy ministry, visiting the sick, or caring for widows, but rather why it is doing so. The focus of the answer will be a strong indicator of how dependent the church is upon God's Word. For example, some churches will emphasize numerical growth or love of neighbors as the basis for ministry. However, the glory of God through obedience to the commands of Scripture ought to drive the work of the church. Within the different ministries of the church, a man pursuing the call of God will be tested and trained. Thus, when ministries exist within the local church because Scripture prescribes them, these ministries reveal a local church whose faith and practice are centered upon Scripture and which is better equipped to give an external call.

A local church with pastors that shepherd and care for God's people

A shepherd loves, guides, protects, and closely involves himself with the sheep. This relationship is what Peter meant when he exhorted the elders to "shepherd the flock of God among you" (1 Peter 5:2). Several implications from this command affect the role shepherds are to play when a local church gives an external call.

First, faithfully shepherding the flock implies a deliberate involvement in the lives of the people, especially those sensing an internal call into the ministry. This kind of involvement is crucial for identifying the desire, gifts, and character a brother should possess to become a shepherd. A shepherd's careful involvement can also identify the desire, gifts, and character of a brother who should be challenged to consider pursuing the ministry but who had not thought of doing so.

Next, the pastors who faithfully shepherd their people model faithful shepherding to those who desire the same work. Peter exhorts the elders to shepherd by "proving to be examples to the flock" (1 Peter 5:3). An aspect of spiritual care for those pursuing ministry in the local church, in addition to their own personal spiritual growth, is their growth in shepherding God's people. A medical student learns best from shadowing a doctor interacting with his or her patients. A law student learns most effectively from witnessing a lawyer practice law. Likewise, a young man desiring to be a shepherd will be best equipped for the task by watching, learning, and imitating his pastor's care of him and others.

Finally, a faithful shepherd instructs his flock in the responsibility it has to test, train, affirm, and send those seeking an external call. A local church will not be willing or even know how to give an external call without careful, deliberate guidance from the pastors regarding this responsibility. A faithful, healthy church is one where those who hold the office of pastor truly shepherd.

A local church with a "regenerate" church membership

Regenerate church membership refers to the covenant members of a local congregation who not only profess to follow Christ, but whose lives testify of their transformed hearts. This distinction may appear redundant or unnecessary, as most evangelicals conclude that entrance into the church comes by profession of faith in Christ. Yet, when we hear reports from the Southern Baptist Convention that fewer than half its recorded members even attend a local church weekly, or from other types of churches where membership is based on political position and levels of influence, not a profession of faith, it is important to make a distinction. There are several implications that necessitate a regenerate church membership in order for a local church to affirm those called into ministry.

Only a born-again believer in Christ can identify and affirm one called to this office of shepherding other believers in the church. Even if a person's father helped build the church or gave large amounts of money to the church, if that person's heart and mind have not been transformed by the gospel, he or she is blind to the basic roles of a church member and will be even more so in the evaluation of the called in the church.

Another implication showing the importance of a regenerate church membership concerns the willingness to be involved in the process of testing, training, affirming, and sending. Church members, recognizing the role they play in the external call, require a godly discernment, a selflessness in giving up others for the advancement of other churches, and a general desire to see local churches healthy and the kingdom of God advance. A heart hardened to Christ and the gospel cannot perform this role and oftentimes labors against it in the church.

A regenerate church membership is even more necessary, and the implications expand, in local churches whose polity is congregational. A pastor-led congregational church expects the members to affirm other members into the church, make important decisions in the church, and be the last line of affirmation for a brother seeking an external call. Thus the external call cannot be accurately given without a local church taking membership seriously and requiring its members to be truly new creatures in Christ (2 Cor. 5:17).

A local church that practices church discipline

Church discipline is the process that a local church initiates towards a member who is found sinning and who shows no signs of genuine repentance. Much like the external call, the recovery of church discipline is desperately needed in the twenty-first-century church. J. L. Dagg would agree, as he wrote, "When discipline leaves the church, Christ goes with it."[5] What would cause Dagg to make such a strong statement about something that is perceived as unloving, unhelpful, and unnecessary to many in the modern church?

The first reason is its biblical basis. God disciplines those he loves and calls his own (Heb. 12:4–8). He tells us to judge ourselves (2 Cor. 13:5; 2 Peter 1:5–10). He instructs us to examine one another in the church and, if necessary, discipline those within it (Matt. 18:15–17; 1 Cor. 5:1–11; 2 Thes. 3:6–15; Gal. 6:1). According to God's design, church discipline is to be a regular part of the life of the church.

The second reason is the benefit for the members of the church. God did not design the Christian life to be pursued individually. God's intention has always been that we have others around us, to "reprove, rebuke, exhort, with great patience and instruction" (2 Tim. 4:2). One of the greatest fallacies in evaluating church discipline is the conclusion that it is unloving, because in actuality it becomes one of the most loving things we can do for a brother or sister in the church blinded to the reality and effects of sin in his or her life. Scripture affirms that church discipline is done to benefit the local church as a whole. Discipline is to be carried out gently, with restoration in mind (Gal. 6:1) and for the sake of the person's eternal soul (1 Cor. 5:1–11). It is to be done to help other members see the seriousness of sin and keep them from falling into it (1 Tim. 5:20). God has designed church discipline to be loving, helpful, and a necessary tool to assist one another to walk in faithfulness to the Savior.

The third reason is an implication that arises from the previous two. Church discipline is essential in order for a local church to be effective in testing, training, affirming, and sending men in the church into the gospel ministry. A willingness to discipline those in sin out of love for them creates a culture in which members will say hard, potentially painful things to other brothers or sisters in the church for their benefit. A willingness to say such things in love is required if a church is to be faithful in giving an external call.

For example, a church must be willing not to affirm and send a brother if it feels that disqualifying issues obligate the church to discourage his pursuit of the ministry. On the other hand, a church must be willing to affirm and send a brother, even if the road chosen will be a great sacrifice or even dangerous. Sending a family into the mission field where persecution certainly awaits them, or affirming a brother to take a $100,000 pay cut from his marketing job to pastor a small church in the country, are decisions that should not be taken lightly. Nevertheless, they are decisions that must be made by a local church that strives to be faithful to God, his Word, and the responsibility to test, train, affirm, and send effectively.

For his purposes, God can use any church that strives to be faithful to the gospel of Jesus Christ. But a local church that pursues faithfulness and health in these four areas will be better equipped to give an external call to those who seek it. In light of our consideration of those who pursue an external call into the ministry and the kind of church that gives it, how do these two entities function practically in the testing, training, affirming, and sending of men within the local church? It is the practical outworking of this process to which we now turn.

How should we proceed with the external call?

IN THIS CHAPTER

Test through real-life circumstances →

Train through deliberate, watchful care →

Affirm by pastors and a local church →

Send with the intent to pray, serve, and support →

In regard to these qualifications, the churches are usually better judges than the individual himself, and must exercise their judgment with prudence and fidelity, under a solemn sense of their accountability, and "lay not careless hands on heads that cannot teach and will not learn."

–Basil Manly, Jr.

It is unwise to assume that someone who has acquired a great deal of knowledge about something is now qualified to do it. The individual excited about skydiving because of the book he just read on it is no more prepared now to skydive than a man is prepared to preach because he heard an excellent sermon. Likewise, I do not assume that, having read the biblical, theological, and philosophical argument of the first four chapters of this book, you are naturally imagining what "testing, training, affirming, and sending" looks like in your particular church. Thus, we have finally arrived at the place where we will consider what these aspects of the external call look like physically and practically in the life of a local church.

We need to be reminded that Acts 13 is simply a picture for us, and that the Bible gives no specific examples of how to test and train appropriately so that local-church pastors and congregations can know how to affirm and send. Many of the following practical suggestions, therefore, come from the efforts made in my own local church that we have found helpful as well as beneficial to those seeking an external call. A helpful guide when approaching a process that is fruitful for your church context is to ensure that a twofold purpose is accomplished: the local church is faithfully served and encouraged, and the individual is tested, trained, affirmed, and sent.

Testing

We know from Paul that God gives some men to the church who are apostles, prophets, evangelists, pastors, and teachers for the equipping and building up of the church (Eph. 4:11–12). The best way to find them is to test those who feel an *internal* calling to this work. A practical definition of testing is the placing of an individual into different real-life circumstances to see how he or she handles them. The best way to test men for the office of pastor, therefore, is to evaluate them in those life circumstances according to the qualifications for this office clearly mapped out for us in Scripture (1 Tim. 3:1–7; Titus 1:5–9). Through these listed characteristics, we can begin to determine whether a young man desiring this work is called, especially through testing his gift to preach and teach. This is a testing that should be carried out visibly in many ways before the congregation.

For example, in my church we have twelve different men who are desiring to test their gifts to preach, preach a psalm on Sunday evenings every summer. This acts not only as an opportunity for them to serve our church, but also as a way for their preaching gifts to be tested before the entire church. We encourage church members to approach each individual after the service to give specific comments of encouragement and critique in a loving, helpful way. A mandatory service review[1] is held after the Sunday evening service and this is attended by the pastors and a few other men who are testing their gifts in order to speak kindly, yet truthfully, into this brother's life about the sermon. Encouragements are given, corrections are made, and suggestions are helpfully submitted for improvement for the next time.

These brothers are also tested when they go and visit church members' homes. Not only are they caring for individual members in going to see them, but they are also being tested in a pastoral way, regarding how patient, kind, gentle, peaceful, respectable, and self-controlled they are. These are all qualities

Paul highlights (1 Tim. 3:1–7; Titus 1:5–9). As a brother visits different members within the church, the pastors either accompany him or informally check to see how the visit went and what fruit seemed to come from it. When a brother who desires the work of a shepherd is confronted with the care of a dying saint in the hospital waiting for a word of comfort, the ground of testing has been significantly plowed.

In the kind providence of God, every portion of an individual's testing works for the good of the local church as a whole. When a brother preaches, he is feeding God's people through his labor in the Word. When a brother disciples another brother in the congregation, he is helping him mature and grow in his faith in Christ. When a brother visits a homebound church member or a member in the hospital, he is caring for the soul of that church member and ultimately serving the pastors and church as a whole. Yet, as these men serve the church in the midst of this testing, they are also beginning to learn those daily labors of a pastor which they cannot learn from a book or class. Consequently, their hands-on training for the ministry has begun.

Training

This is testing that becomes a little more deliberate. This stage is reached when the pastors of the church have, to some degree, identified gifts reflected from 1 Timothy 3:1–7 in a man who needs to be more deliberately tested and trained through practical experience. This is where a brother begins to play a more active role in the leadership of the church by, for example, regularly teaching a class, leading services, or preaching for a whole month on Sunday evenings. This is someone the pastors begin to trust, sending him to the hospital to visit on his own or exposing him more to the decisions and directions of the church. This is someone who is involved in evaluating the sermons and the services every week. In all these efforts, these brothers are being trained for ministry and the members of the church continue to be served, encouraged, and cared for through their efforts.

At a recent commissioning service for missionaries of my congregation, I exhorted a family who had been through this stage of the process in this way:

> You [husband and wife] have been in many of our homes and us in yours. We have had the joy of fellowship with you. You have served our church in so many ways. You [wife] have cared for our children as you have faithfully cared for your own. You have modeled a Christ-like attitude through a very difficult family schedule. You [husband] have faithfully preached and taught God's Word to us. You have helped several people spiritually grow through your discipleship efforts. You [husband] have helped lead our public gatherings and have used your pastoral experience to help the pastors think through some difficult issues. However, as we fellowshipped together and served with you both, something else was happening—you were being tested and trained before our eyes for the work to which you felt called. By God's grace, he has allowed our church the joy of Christian fellowship with you through that time to put us in a place to affirm you.

This is just one example of what the training of an individual looks like. It is centered within the local church. It is led by the pastors. The members of that local church are the most affected. Ultimately, it allows the local church as a whole to be put into a position to affirm the man's gifts and calling.

Affirming

Once the pastors and leaders have had adequate time to test and train a brother pursuing the ministry, the time comes to either affirm him or not. If the pastors feel, through much discussion, that a brother does possess an internal call, in my church we then recommend him to the congregation, so that they can evaluate him also. Because much of this testing and training is carried out visibly before the people and with the people, members of the congregation have, hopefully, now been informed enough to make their own decision. This has resulted in very helpful and fruitful discussions in our members' meetings. If there are no concerns about the pastors' recommendation, the church comes back after a month of praying to vote.

This affirmation can come in different ways. It may be an affirmation for a brother to serve as an assistant pastor in our church. It may be an affirmation because someone is leaving to pursue a ministry position. It may be to affirm a couple who are going to the mission field. It may be to affirm someone whom the church is sending to plant a church elsewhere in the city. Regardless of the scenario, the decision to ordain a brother as a pastor or missionary is the final step before we send him with the full support and external call of our local church.

Here is an excerpt from a public statement made to my church about a family pursuing missionary work. It reveals the kind of scrutiny that should accompany our responsibility:

> I have had one-on-one meetings with them to discuss their marriage, family, educational challenges, and struggles with sin. The pastors have discussed their situation on numerous occasions. We have had several public discussions about this family at our members' meetings. Yet they still sit here desiring our affirmation because in all those discussions, we as a church have felt convinced, though the road they face will be hard, that this is the work the Lord has for them.

This statement was designed to remind the congregation of the process this family had engaged in, but also that the time had come to affirm them.

Similar statements were made to the congregation of a brother pursuing pastoral ministry in a local church:

> I have had one-on-one meetings with this man and his wife about their marriage. We have watched him shepherd his wife and children, faithfully demonstrating a faithful management of his household. He has demonstrated that he is gifted to teach and preach through his faithful labor of the Word among us. He has been in many of your homes, displaying his love for you and your souls. He has been to see many of you in the hospital, bringing the comfort of the gospel to your time of need. He has conducted himself in our church with kindness, patience, gentleness, self-control, and a moral character that is above reproach. Though the struggles of pastoral ministry will challenge every area we have tested and trained him in, we are confident of the Lord's hand upon him for this work.

Regardless of your church polity, every local congregation must arrive at this point of affirmation before it can send a man appropriately. Once an individual has been tested, trained, and affirmed by the leaders and congregation, we then do what God has called us to do—send him out.

Sending

It can be a complicated and involved process to send a man out. Whether it is someone pursuing a pastorate or missions, or simply the step to pursue theological education, as a church we are, in sending him out, committing to several things: to pray regularly for him, possibly give wisdom and pastoral oversight regarding where he should go, and then be in regular contact with him while on the field. The church may need to make a commitment to support him financially, especially if he is going as a missionary to the field but is not funded by any person or organization. For an individual pursuing theological education there needs to be oversight of his faithful involvement in a local church that is committed to continuing the process of the external call your church has begun. Sending is not the end of the process, but rather the beginning of a new commitment that a local church gives to those who have been tested, trained, affirmed, and sent out.

The sending process is seen most tangibly in a special church service. These kinds of services are most commonly described as "ordination" or "commissioning" services. The individual has already been affirmed, so this acts as the more formal effort of acknowledging his gifts and calling. The service could contain vows that are repeated by those being sent as well as by the congregation that is sending them.[2] The sermon that is preached should point to the biblical qualifications required by an individual to receive an external call, the task of those biblically called, or the responsibility of the local church in assuming the authority to affirm. The services can contain a variety of very encouraging aspects that instruct, encourage, and challenge the individual and the congregation.

The most important aspect of the service is when the pastors and leaders of the church lay their hands on the individual and pray for him and the ministry to which he is being called. This embraces the model given to us by the church in Antioch (Acts 13:3). The laying-on of hands and praying are not some mystical transfer that changes the individual; they simply mark the conclusion of this process of being tested, trained, and affirmed by the pastors and members of the congregation, and represent the authority Christ gave to his church to send those who have been called and properly examined. Basil Manly, Jr., one of the founding fathers of the Southern Baptist Theological Seminary, emphasized the responsibility of the local church in identifying those who qualify as ministers of the gospel, and how the laying-on of hands symbolizes that authority: "In regard to these qualifications, the churches are usually better judges than the individual himself, and must exercise their judgment with prudence and fidelity, under a solemn sense of their accountability, and 'lay not careless hands on heads that cannot teach and will not learn.'"[3]

Here is one way I have explained the laying-on of hands in a service of commission: "In a few moments, we will do what the church in Antioch did in Acts 13:3—we will lay hands on each of you and pray, sealing our affirmation of you to pursue these opportunities of ministry by God's grace." The laying-on of hands is not to be seen as some supernatural event by which the individuals prayed for are now more ready for the task than before. Nevertheless, we must understand the significance of what is happening as the pastors and leaders lay their hands on the individuals and pray. They pray for their continual fruitfulness as they minister the gospel. They pray for their faithfulness to the gospel in the proclamation of God's Word. They pray that the men and their families will be protected from the evil one. They pray for their growing zeal for the work to which they have been called. They pray for Christ's presence by his Spirit to be with them. They pray for the purity of their lives and their hatred of sin. They pray for their faithfulness in loving their wives as Christ loved the church and in shepherding their children. They pray that God's kingdom will continue to advance because of their willingness to answer the call. This is significant because God is able to empower those who answer this call to do exactly what is prayed for. Just like the church in Antioch, we, by faith, believe that as we send these men out, so the Spirit also sends them out to walk in the ways we have prayed publicly and corporately for them (Acts 13:3–4).

Finally, a practical note on how to proceed depending on the particular role you play within your local church. I would like to address three groups of people: the pastor(s), those sensing the call to the ministry, and regular faithful church members.

The pastor(s)

The vision to establish this process within your local church starts with you. It takes a pastor to recognize a pastor. In the same way you look with a keen eye for the discouraged, hurting sheep in your flock, look for those who seem to be gifted as shepherds. Look past the apparent immaturities and discern those who may have a special gift from God to teach his Word and care for his people. In the absence of a formal process, take these individuals to the hospital with you; let them tag along when you visit the homebound. When you feel it is time, let them teach a small-group Bible study where you can observe them in that role. Begin teaching your congregation about their role in this process. Fellow laborers of the gospel, this process begins with us. You will not include this task into your already busy life of ministry if you do not see the need for it and that God has appointed us the vision casters of this responsibility in our churches.

Those sensing the call

If you are one who desires the work of a pastor or missionary, Paul says that you desire a fine work (1 Tim. 3:1). Yet your responsibility is not simply to rely on your internal call to develop your individual gifts, but to place yourself under the authority of the local church and trust that God will work through the pastors and believers in that congregation to affirm your internal call with an external call. Take every opportunity to serve and care for the souls of the people in your church. Take every opportunity you are given to teach or preach. Humbly serve the church in the smallest of ways, trusting that God is preparing you for every future opportunity to minister the gospel to someone. Trust that God is at work not only in you as you pursue this calling, but also in your local church to affirm that which you feel called to do.

Regular, faithful church members

It needs to be acknowledged that the overwhelming majority of church members do not feel a call to the ministry. If you do not feel this call, your responsibility is to continue to do what a faithful church member does. Invest in and pour your life into the people of the church, so that when the time comes to affirm someone for the ministry, you are well informed. When a young, inexperienced brother is given an opportunity to teach a Bible study or preach on a Sunday evening, take the time to go and attentively listen. Approach him afterwards and encourage him with those things you thought he did well and lovingly correct him where he can improve. Put your personal preferences aside regarding the kind of person you like as a preacher, and embrace the opportunity of helping someone else to grow and learn from his experience. If a young man calls, asking if he can come to visit you, love and encourage him as he makes the effort to learn and to minister to you. God has a specific role for every member of the church to play in testing, training, affirming, and sending those called into the ministry. Will you see the significance and be faithful in playing your role?

There are certainly other ways to proceed in testing, training, affirming, and sending than those described in this chapter. The main question is, will you proceed? The main reason I hear for why churches decline to pursue this task is the inability to know how to move forward practically in it. May the outworking of the external call as set out in this chapter spark ideas of ways in which this process can become a reality for you, your church, and those in your church who await your efforts to test, train, affirm, and send them.

What is at stake with the external call?

IN THIS CHAPTER

The lives of individual Christians are endangered →

The health and well-being of local churches are threatened →

The effectiveness of theological education is jeopardized →

The glory and name of Christ are at stake →

It is a fearful calamity to a man to miss his calling, and to the church upon whom he imposes himself, his mistake involves an affliction of the most grievous kind.

–Charles H. Spurgeon

The finest biography on the great eighteenth-century evangelist George Whitefield is arguably Arnold Dallimore's two-volume work. In it, Dallimore captures the life and times of this great historical figure, and how Whitefield's love for Christ and the souls of men compelled him to preach bold, powerful, and oftentimes controversial sermons and moved him to speak against many social injustices as he traveled throughout America and Great Britain.

Another part of Whitefield's mission that is largely overlooked, but which Dallimore develops brilliantly, is Whitefield's zeal for speaking against the unconverted and unfaithful who were filling pulpits all across New England in the eighteenth century. In a journal entry written after Whitefield had attended a service in New York, he explains why he chose to take on such a controversial issue: "... felt my heart almost bleed within me, to consider what blind guides were sent forth into her. If I have any regard for the honour of Christ and the good of souls, I must lift up my voice like a trumpet, and shew how sadly our Church ministers are fallen away from the doctrines of the Reformation."[1]

As Whitefield shook pulpits across New England with the powerful preaching of the gospel, he also shook these wolves in sheep's clothing who regularly manned many of those pulpits. Whitefield's efforts were met with great hostility and opposition, as Arnold Dallimore accurately observed: "In the apathy of the times, the principle 'A converted minister is best, but an unconverted one cannot fail to do some good' had become almost everywhere accepted."[2] For this reason, Whitefield attacked this destructive pattern in the church with the same zeal with which he challenged the lost souls in the fields of open-air preaching, because he knew what was at stake if men filled pulpits and were charged to shepherd God's people when they had not been called to do so.

In considering this great responsibility of the local church with regard to the external call, we must realize what is at stake if the local church fails in this task. Before we determine some of the destructive effects of the local church failing in this area, it must be acknowledged what is not at stake. Jesus declared that he will build his church and the gates of Hades will not prevail over it (Matt. 16:18). God's work of redemption is a finished work in the sufficient sacrifice of Jesus Christ (Heb. 1:3; 10:14). God chose a people before the foundation of the world (Eph. 1:4) from every tribe, tongue, people, and nation—a people that has been purchased by the blood of the Lamb and will be brought into the kingdom of God as the gospel is preached among all the nations (Rev. 5:9–10). These truths are biblical certainties that are not contingent on our faithfulness to the external call, but upon the sovereign purposes and perfect will of our faithful God.

Yet God accomplishes these purposes by working in and through his people. Because of this, much is at stake in the lives of individual Christians, in the well-being of local churches, in the effectiveness of theological education, and ultimately for the glory and name of Christ, if local churches refuse to be faithful to the external call. These four areas of risk warn the local church to engage and persevere in the testing, training, affirming, and sending of the called into gospel ministry.

The lives of individual Christians

Different groups of Christians are harmed by the church's failure in this task. The most obvious category of Christians negatively affected consists of those who trust themselves to a shepherd who is unwilling or unable to shepherd. Yet those most seriously affected are Christians who seek to pursue ministry but should not.

I love football, especially the National Football League (NFL). I love to watch games, and when I watch them, a desire to get out there and play wells up within me. If I allowed myself, I could become convinced that I could actually play successfully. What do you think would happen to me if I actually played in a professional football game? I would be crushed! Regardless of how much I thought I was ready to play, one head-on collision with a three-hundred-pound lineman would jolt me back into reality. The harm and injury I would face from a hit like that could be avoided if someone observed and stated the obvious to me: "You're too old, too small, and do not possess the gifts to survive playing in a professional football game."

Similarly, those who shepherd God's people but are not gifted and called to do so risk much harm to the sheep but also painful results for themselves. We had a young man in our church who desired pastoral office and demonstrated some gifts that led him in that direction. Unfortunately, certain aspects of his life—primarily his difficult and fragile marriage—concerned the pastors, which led to our discouragement of his pursuit of ministry. This man called a meeting informing us of his pursuit of an associate-pastor position with the request that we would affirm him for the position. As painful as it was, in good conscience we could not recommend him to the congregation at that time because of these growing marriage difficulties. He rejected our counsel, accepted the ministry position, and left our church with resentment towards those of us who felt that ministry would only magnify his marriage problems. Unfortunately, those marriage problems escalated through the pressures of ministry, and his wife took their children and left him. Though our relationship with the man has since been mended, his relationship with his wife has not. The local church must take this responsibility seriously, realize what is at stake, and caution any individual unable to evaluate his own fragile circumstances.

The well-being of local churches

George Whitefield pronounced a death sentence upon churches that contained unfaithful shepherds: "The reason why congregations have been so dead is because they have dead men preaching to them."[3] There is much at stake in the well-being of local churches who have dead men preaching to them, prideful men guiding them, and greedy men abusing them. Anyone who questions how badly an unfaithful shepherd can harm sheep has never experienced the pain of a pastor abusing his position to embezzle money or sexually pursue a vulnerable married woman in his congregation. Scandals such as these not only painfully harm the individuals involved, but also wound the local churches as a whole to a potentially unrecoverable condition.

I once served on the staff of a large local church that had a pastor with some questionable financial practices. If anyone confronted the pastor's practices, that person was often fired. As a result, most tried to ignore the rumors and just focused on their areas of ministry. Two years after I left that church, the pastor was investigated and was exposed as having traded hundreds of thousands of dollars of the church's money on the stock market and lost it all. To make matters worse, the pastor who then replaced him was caught in an adulterous affair one year later and left the ministry. The harm these two men have caused this local church is incalculable!

Disqualifying sin can creep into the lives of the most faithful of pastors. Those in gospel ministry of any kind receive the front-line attacks of the enemy and must be on guard at all times and surrounded by faithful men for accountability. For this reason, a local church that sees the great risk that can come if an unfaithful shepherd is given this kind of authority, power, influence, and position will be a local church that does its part in protecting other local churches. This protection is best accomplished by a local church being faithful in only affirming and sending those who truly have been called.

The effectiveness of theological education

Seminaries and Bible colleges are such a wonderful tool for those called by God, and they are capable of accomplishing so much in the educating of future pastors and missionaries. Yet, as gifted as the professors are, and as numerous as are the resources poured into theological education, they still cannot replace this unique role of the local church regarding the external call. As mentioned in Chapter 2, institutions of theological education have wrongfully been given this ultimate responsibility, and when they assume this role, these institutions are distracted from their primary purpose.

For example, I once had a meeting with the supervisor of the applied ministry program of a seminary and asked him why so few hours were dedicated to the practical side of ministry, presuming that the seminary had accepted the responsibility to train as well as educate. The supervisor's answer was that increasing the requirements of applied ministry meant that they would have to decrease the requirements of other areas within their students' already loaded schedules. The failure of the local church to assume the responsibility of training practically those pursuing gospel ministry puts unneeded pressure upon institutions of theological education, with the result that they are not able to completely focus on what they do best—teaching the original languages, plumbing the depths of systematic theology, and covering an enormous amount of church history in a short period of time.

The local church should be working alongside theological

institutions to prepare gospel ministers; without this marriage an unnecessary and harmful expectation is certain to remain upon these institutions. Yet, when these two entities work together, fruitful training is certain to come. A powerful, balanced example of this relationship in my church was two young single brothers attending the local seminary and faithfully serving and submitting themselves to the local church. During the week, they were immersed in studying Greek and Hebrew, yet they spent Sundays effectively loving and teaching the children's Sunday-school class. During the week, they were bombarded with the need to write systematic-theology and church-history papers late at night, yet spent their free time caring for widows and visiting the sick.

For others with no local presence of a theological institution, this balance could be met by a season at seminary followed by a season serving within a local church. Regardless of the scenario, this fruitful result is achievable, but it must come from the local church accepting its role and theological institutions submitting to the local church. The maximum effectiveness of these theological institutions is at stake when local churches do not assume this God-given role.

The glory and name of Christ

God's plan is that the corporate witness of the redeemed in the local church display the gospel of Jesus Christ to a lost and dying world. This corporate witness will be distorted if shepherds without the unique call of God are placed in positions of shepherding. Christians following a shepherd not called by God can be led into believing false teaching, living unruly lives, and losing sight of the intended purpose of the local church—to display the gospel until Christ returns for his bride.

Additionally, the furtherance of the gospel among the nations will be hindered if missionaries not equipped for the task go to the field. Many of us have heard the unfortunate testimonies of missionaries who go to the field with little examination and accountability and are harmfully affected by the pagan cultures in which they are immersed. Missionaries become discouraged, soften on essentials of doctrine, and experience the intense spiritual attacks of the enemy that often leave them ineffective and muddy the clear waters of the gospel. The local church's faithfulness in testing, training, affirming, and sending pastors and missionaries will directly promote the progress of the gospel, the corporate witness of the church, and ultimately the renown and glory of our Savior and King, Jesus.

The biblical command and purpose of the external call has been the key component of this argument to motivate local churches to engage in this calling. Let the warning of this chapter, however, act as a sobering reminder of what is truly at stake if the local church fails to recover this essential responsibility God has given his people.

Conclusion

IN THIS CHAPTER

A real-life example ➔

The reward for faithfulness ➔

Is it not worth all our labors and suffering ... to hear one spiritual child say, Lord, this is the minister by whom I believed: Another, this is he, by whom I was edified, established, and comforted. This is the man that resolved my doubts, quickened my dying affections, reduced my soul, when wandering from the truth!

–John Flavel

The argument laid down in these pages is not just biblical, philosophical, and instructive, but it is also the commitment and conviction of my local church—Auburndale Baptist Church in Louisville, Kentucky—which has experienced the joys and sorrows of assuming this responsibility with the external call. To conclude, I thought it would be helpful to describe an example from my congregation that provides, though imperfectly, a real-life illustration.

A young married Christian man with two children moved to Louisville to attend seminary. He had come from a very solid, healthy, and faithful local church, where he had been discipled, taught well, and given opportunities to serve. In the midst of sensing an internal call, he approached the elders of the church to inquire of their thoughts regarding his leaving and attending seminary. They acknowledged certain gifts he possessed that would point to some kind of pastoral ministry, and took further steps to observe his life, gifts, and effectiveness as a teacher. After this period of time, he left with the full support and affirmation of this local church to attend seminary and pursue pastoral ministry.

He and his family arrived in Louisville and decided to settle at and commit to my church. Early on, he and his family showed a deep commitment to the church. Whether it was serving in the nursery or through hospitality, discipling others, evangelism, taking his family to visit the sick and widows, or cutting down trees around the church, this brother demonstrated a love for Christ, a love for God's people, and a strong desire for the work of a pastor. Because of this desire and the faithfulness he showed, we allowed him opportunities to preach and teach. Our pastors and congregation grew in encouragement as we saw the fruitfulness of his service and his personal spiritual growth as a follower of Christ.

However, our maturing in Christ does not come without struggles and the attacks of the enemy. The stress of working a job, managing a full load of seminary, and juggling family as well as church life, wore him down and he struggled with discouragement. He sought out the pastors for care and encouragement, and modeled the way a brother should seek spiritual care when dark times come. Eventually, he resumed his labor in our church with a seemingly greater zeal than before. By his grace, God had used this dark time of struggle to mature this brother in special ways that caused him to have a greater love for the gospel, a greater burden for the struggles of our people, and a greater capacity to shepherd God's people in our church.

As a result, he was officially put forward and affirmed as a pastor of our congregation. During this time, his fruitfulness as a preacher and shepherd only grew. He was wise, insightful, and discerning in many difficult and challenging situations that the pastors faced and led the congregation through, including the first painful disciplining and eventual removal of a church member. His faithfulness in serving alongside us as pastors, and the sweet fellowship with him and his family, were undeniable reminders of his internal calling and of why God has appointed a plurality of pastors/elders to lead, care, guide, and shepherd God's people by his Word in a local church.

After his faithful pastoral service for a time in our congregation and his eventual completion of theological education, he was sent with the full support and affirmation of our church to serve as senior pastor of another church. He was sent with sadness because of our loss, yet with great joy because of what that church gained. He continues to serve faithfully in that church today. As a church, we continue to pray for him regularly, support him in whatever way he needs, and rejoice in the privilege of being a part of all the Lord is doing through this brother's faithful gospel-centered ministry.

In 2009, we sent another brother from our church, who had been through the same testing, training, affirming, and sending process, to go and serve alongside him as his associate. In God's kind providence, one of the many ways this former pastor of our church had labored while with us was in the discipling, mentoring, and instructing of this very brother who now serves as his associate.

One of the greatest joys that we as pastors, as well as our entire congregation, now experience through similar scenarios is seeing our conviction for faithful gospel-centered preaching, the tireless shepherding of God's people, and the building of Christ's kingdom outside our local church, multiply through these brothers we test, train, affirm, and send into gospel ministry. Without a doubt, struggles and sorrows accompany this task. Yet we labor in this task because we desire that shepherds and the sheep cared for by them in the local church around the world experience what the great Puritan pastor John Flavel captured so powerfully:

> O Brethren! Who would not study and pray, spend and be spent, in the service of such a bountiful Master! Is it not worth all our labours and sufferings, to come with all those souls we instrumentally begat to Christ: and all that we edified, established, confirmed, and comforted in the way to heaven; and say, Lord, here am I, and the children thou hast given me? To hear one spiritual

child say, Lord, this is the minister by whom I believed: Another, this is he, by whom I was edified, established, and comforted. This is the man that resolved my doubts, quickened my dying affections, reduced my soul, when wandering from the truth![1]

For this reason, let us assume this responsibility of testing, training, affirming, and sending into gospel ministry those whom our bountiful Master has entrusted to us. Let us do so to be faithful, but also to look forward with great anticipation to that glorious day when our Chief Shepherd will appear and we are able to celebrate with all those who receive that unfading crown of glory promised to all the called, faithful, and steadfast shepherds of the Lord Jesus Christ (1 Peter 5:4).

APPENDIX 1. PASTORAL INTERNSHIP TEMPLATE

This template was designed with Donald Whitney to work in conjunction with the Applied Ministry courses of the Southern Baptist Theological Seminary. It shows one possible scenario of how to partner a pastoral internship with a theological institution. It is not, however, necessary to do so.

[Name of church]
Pastoral Internship
(In cooperation with the SBTS Applied
Ministry syllabus and handbook)

Purpose and benefit

The purpose of this internship is to provide an atmosphere within a local church to train, equip, and affirm men for pastoral ministry. There are five potential benefits in considering this internship:

First, the benefit of a supportive and loving environment of a local church that assumes responsibility for the care, training, and education of the intern.

Second, the receiving of practical understanding and training for the essential areas of pastoral ministry within the local church.

Third, the gaining of an official church position approved by the church that can go on a résumé reflecting ministry experience.

Fourth, the opportunity for a local congregation to affirm an individual's gifts and calling.

Fifth, the exposure to a pastor's daily schedule to help an individual evaluate the pastoral nature of his calling.

Duration
January through April *or* May through August *or* September through December

Compensation
There is no salary for this position.

Hourly requirements
Approximately 11 hours (weekly).
   (Wed: 3 p.m.–8 p.m.; Sun: 9 a.m.–12 noon; 5 p.m.–8 p.m.)
   (Flexible according to the intern's needs and availability.)

Learning objectives

GENERAL OBJECTIVES
- Sermon and worship-service planning and preparation
- Disciplined prayer life
- Pastoral care: hospitals, visitation, member care, and membership interviews
- Public-worship service involvement and evaluation
- Funerals and weddings
- Leadership meetings (pastors, staff, deacons, committees, etc.)
- Essentials of administration
- Monthly report to the congregation on personal progress
- In addition to SBTS Applied Ministry requirements, two additional books to read and discuss with pastor or field supervisor (paid for by the church)
- In addition to SBTS Applied Ministry requirements, two additional (5-page) papers to write: theological implications on practical ministry issues

Field supervisor for SBTS requirement
Senior pastor

➡ Test, train, affirm & send into ministry

Secondary supervisor
Other pastors or staff

Internship weekly schedule (flexible)

WEDNESDAY

3 p.m.–4 p.m.—Meet with pastor: discuss book/paper; time of instruction with learning objectives/personal goals.

4 p.m.–5 p.m.—Worship-service planning with the pastors

5 p.m.–7 p.m.—Staff meeting/administration and bookkeeping/Bible study

7 p.m.–8 p.m.—Bible study

SUNDAY

9 a.m.–9:30 a.m.—Meet at church/pray/prepare for adult Sunday morning Bible study

9:30 a.m.–10:30 a.m.—Attend adult Sunday morning Bible study

10:45 a.m.—12 noon—Morning gathering

5 p.m.–5:30 p.m.—Monthly meetings: pastors/deacons/committees/membership interviews, etc.

5:30 p.m.–6 p.m.—Prepare for evening gathering

6 p.m.–7 p.m.—Evening gathering

7:15 p.m.–8 p.m.—Service review

APPENDIX 2. SERVICE REVIEW EVALUATION

I was first exposed to this idea through my friend and mentor Mark Dever and the ministry of Capitol Hill Baptist Church in Washington, D.C. I have tweaked it over the years, but very little originated with me.

Setting

Service review takes place as a round-table discussion with one primary facilitator to evaluate the public gatherings for that Lord's Day. It works best to have this time fifteen minutes after the evening service, with a duration of forty-five minutes to one hour. There are two main benefits: First, everyone is already at church to meet before going home for the day. Second, the gatherings for that Lord's Day are fresh on everyone's minds and hearts, which produces a more engaged evaluation. This time also provides wives and children with the option to stay and fellowship with one another while the men meet. Sensitivity to families waiting is why this meeting should last one hour maximum. Anyone is invited to attend, but primarily those men who participate in leading and preaching in the public gathering, or aspire to do so. Those leading and preaching that day, as well as current pastoral interns, are required to attend.

Purpose

The primary role of service review is twofold: First, it is a safeguard to maintain biblical fidelity within the public gatherings of the church. Second, it is a tool to cultivate the skill of giving and receiving sincere, helpful, and godly criticism, which does not come naturally. It must be learned, taught, and molded into believers. Within these two chief purposes, there are several other purposes to be accomplished in setting this time aside for evaluation:

- To provide an opportunity to speak words of

encouragement as well as correction if needed into the lives of those who led and preached in the public gathering;

- To create a culture of evaluating the public gatherings, not by preference or style, but biblically, theologically, pastorally, and practically;
- To create an environment to evaluate critically what is important and what is not important in regard to sermons and services;
- To create an environment for those participating and observing to learn, grow, and mature in the various roles discussed;
- To learn discernment in what are helpful, instructive comments—and what are not;
- To create an environment of humility, trust, fellowship, and openness with our lives with those present.

Process

The facilitator's role is much like a moderator or chairman. He is to keep the discussion progressing in a helpful direction and protect the group from digressing in a negative manner. The facilitator asks a question about the service or sermon and goes around the table soliciting thoughts and comments about that particular question. Here are some examples:

- Did the service run on one continuous theme that led into the preaching of the Word?
- What encouraging comments do you have for those who led the service?
- What could have been done better?
- Any theological concerns with the songs chosen?
- Did the congregation seem to sing well? Why or why not?

- What was one truth prayed in the service that was particularly meaningful to you?
- Was the Lord's Table administered in a biblically appropriate way?
- Were there any distractions that need to be mentioned?
- What connections did you see between the Scripture readings and the sermon?
- What did you learn in the exposition of the text that you didn't notice before?
- What application from the sermon was particularly meaningful to you?
- Was there any portion of the sermon that you would suggest amending or condensing?
- Were there any errors spoken, or clarifications that need to be made by those who led or preached?

The facilitator can also use this time to have a short discussion about a topic if he feels it would benefit the group. Topics could include approaches to preaching a certain text, factors in determining songs, methods of applying texts edifyingly and faithfully, good templates to think through when praying publicly, and techniques for communicating effectively (e.g., voice inflection). These are useful conversations to have with those leading and preaching, and with those aspiring to do so in your congregation.

This approach should leave those involved challenged to think through different issues in regard to the public gatherings of the church, but ultimately this time should encourage those who labored in leading and preaching, unless a particularly poor job was done. If you find these meetings have a feeling more of criticism than mutual edification, you need to consider whether the meeting has taken too critical a direction and what adjustments need to be made.

APPENDIX 3. THE EXTERNAL CALL (ACTS 13:1–3)

(A sermon preached at Auburndale Baptist Church, Louisville, Kentucky, December 14, 2008. A Commissioning Service for two families: One being sent to the mission field, the other to be the Senior Pastor of a local church.)

Introduction

There is arguably no equal to Charles Bridges' assessment of the call of God on someone's life and the responsibility of those involved. In his book *The Christian Ministry*, he clearly places the responsibility of one's call into the ministry upon the conscience of the individual *and* the local church to which that man is committed. Bridges calls this evaluation process the internal and external call of God:

> The *external call* is a commission received from and recognized by the Church, not indeed qualifying the minister, but accrediting him, whom God had internally and suitably qualified. This call communicates therefore only official authority. The *internal call* is the voice and power of the Holy Spirit, directing the will and the judgment, and conveying personal qualifications. Both calls, however—though essentially distinct in their character and source—are indispensable for the exercise of our commission.

Bridges is saying that, for an individual to know he is called of God to serve in the ministry, there must be an *internal call*, which is the desire within the man to do the work of the ministry and his own conviction that he has been gifted and empowered by God's Spirit to do so.

However, there must also be an *external call*, which is simply the affirmation from the local church that this person possesses the gifts and godly character suitable for a Christian minister.

Bridges, Spurgeon, and many other godly men whom God used in the past to raise up those called into the ministry, all agree that both the internal and external calls are important for a person to possess to enter into the work of the ministry.

Unfortunately, this process is mostly lost today, but this morning we should as a church consider this great responsibility not only as shown through the counsel of Bridges, but also because it seems to be how the early church and those throughout church history operated, as they recognized, affirmed, and sent those whom God was clearly calling.

Last week, we referenced special relationships between those who go and those who stay. Luther Rice described this as "rope holding." When someone is lowered into a well or cave, someone else must hold the rope, otherwise the person cannot be lowered. If the rope holder at any time drops the rope, the person in the well cannot be brought back up. This is a picture of what it means for the local church to send missionaries to the field and support them continually until their work is done and they are safely brought back home.

Luther Rice held the rope for Adoniram Judson, Andrew Fuller held the rope for William Carey, and these two families sit here this morning because they are grabbing the rope that we as a church are extending to them to take from us as we send one to the mission field and the other into the pastorate. We will consider what that looks like for us as a church in a few moments, but before we do that, let us consider arguably the best example of this in Scripture, which is when the church in Antioch affirms and sends Saul and Barnabas into the work they have been set apart by God to do. Our base passage we are going to work from this morning is this example we find at the beginning of Acts 13.

Let me set the context of where we are stepping into the book of Acts. Jesus has come, lived a perfect life, died on the cross, risen from the dead three days later and, in this accomplished work, purchased salvation from sins and God's wrath with his own blood. Therefore, all who call upon Christ in faith, repent, and give their lives to Him will receive salvation. The book of Acts is the result of this gospel (good news) of Jesus saving sinners being preached by his followers and his church being built.

Chapter 13 marks a turning point in Acts. The first twelve chapters focus mostly on Peter, but the remaining chapters focus on Paul. In the first twelve chapters the focus was on the Jerusalem and Judean church being established. The rest of Acts is focused on the spread of the Gentile church throughout the world. Luke shows us how this sovereign purpose of God in building his church continues as Saul and Barnabas return from Jerusalem to now be officially commissioned for God's purposes by the church in Antioch.

> Now there were at Antioch, in the church that was there, prophets and teachers: Barnabas, and Simeon who was called Niger, and Lucius of Cyrene, and Manaen who had been brought up with Herod the tetrarch, and Saul. While they were ministering to the Lord and fasting, the Holy Spirit said, "Set apart for Me Barnabas and Saul for the work to which I have called them." Then, when they had fasted and prayed and laid their hands on them, they sent them away.
>
> Acts 13:1–3

Let us consider the biblical warrant for the external call, then determine our responsibility to it as a congregation.

The external call of God (vv. 1–3)

The external call of God can only be given by the church, and any effort to place this great responsibility on anyone or anything else risks the health and well-being of local churches and ultimately the witness of Christ. The external call has practically vanished in the twentieth and now the twenty-first century, as many students I know just on the campus of the Southern Baptist Theological Seminary have admitted to me that their home church wasn't involved (or as involved as it could have been) in their decision to pursue ministry.

It is now time for the local church again to embrace this enormous responsibility to test, train, affirm, and send young pastors and missionaries into the ministry by deliberately examining their gifts and characters. This is not only the local church's call today, but has been the responsibility of the church from the beginning, as we see the church in Antioch embracing this responsibility and being faithful to it. The church in Antioch is a great example and picture for us to better understand the external call in its relation to the local church in our day.

Centered on the Local Church (v. 1)

We see in verse 1 the sole presence of the church at Antioch. No presence of seminaries or mission organizations. This is not to say that seminaries and mission organizations are not very helpful and ordained by God. However, what I want us to observe this morning is that, in the early church, the testing, training, affirming and sending of pastors and missionaries was the sole responsibility of the local church and the pastors, leaders, and believers found there. We see in verse 1 the church at Antioch and we see their leaders. The prophets and teachers mentioned in verse 1 were the early church pastors and leaders. This is the central platform through which God reveals his will for Saul and Barnabas—through the other pastors and believers of the church in Antioch.

Recognized by the Pastors (vv. 2–3)

We see these leaders doing what they normally would do, as verse 2 reveals they were ministering to the Lord and fasting. In other words, they were doing the work of the church in preaching and teaching God's Word and shepherding the church and being deliberately prayerful about it. Let's remember what fasting is. Fasting is the purposeful setting aside of eating to concentrate on spiritual issues, predominantly through prayer. We see it is in the faithfulness of these leaders that the Holy Spirit reveals in verse 2 God's will for Saul and Barnabas. They are to be "Set apart for Me ... for the work to which I have called them" (v. 2).

Let's consider the guidance of God in this decision. First and foremost, they certainly had the message of the Holy Spirit in verse 2, which was unique to the establishment of the early church. But let's not forget that they also had the fruitfulness of Saul and Barnabas's previous labor. At the end of Acts 11, Saul and Barnabas came to the church at Antioch and they fellowshipped for an entire year (11:26), met with the church, and cared for them. The church and its leaders had the evidence of God's call on their life because of the fruitfulness of their past labor among them.

Therefore, we see that the church are able to affirm them not only by God's guidance by his Spirit, but also by their past fruitful labor, all in the wisdom of God through their continual fasting and praying. We see the leaders lay their hands on them to affirm them in this call (v. 3), which is not just the affirmation of the leaders, but also of the entire church, which we see in Acts 6 and later in Acts 14.

When colleges send people to recruit for their basketball team, they don't send their baseball or football coaches. They don't even send one of their basketball players. They send one of the coaches who has, first of all, demonstrated ability in playing basketball in the past, and also has shown a level of evaluating other talent by his or her maturity in the knowledge of the game. In the same way, it is a pastor who initially recognizes the potential calling of a young man for him to be tested and trained for the observance of the congregation.

AFFIRMED BY THE LOCAL CHURCH (V. 3)

As we consider the Antioch church, we see that the church and its leaders have been able to watch Saul and Barnabas's lives, see fruitful ministry in this particular church, and have sought the Lord's guidance. Now they officially apply the external call of God upon Saul and Barnabas as they lay their hands on them in affirmation (on behalf of the church; v. 3); then, at the end of verse 3, "they sent them away." Also notice the Spirit's working through the church: The church sends them in verse 3, but verse 4 then says that the Spirit sent them. The church's involvement in their ministry didn't stop at their sending, for as Saul and Barnabas returned from their efforts they "gathered the church together, [and] began to report all things that God had done with them" (Acts 14:27).

All of this was to lead the leaders (prophets/teachers) and the church, by the Holy Spirit, to play some role in giving the external call to Saul and Barnabas to do the work to which God had called them. How do we measure the importance of this affirmation from the Antioch church? It resulted in God continuing to build his church through Gentiles hearing the gospel and the church being built throughout the Roman province and world.

The responsibility of the local church

Not only is this event in Acts 13 simply a picture for us, but also it gives no specific examples of how to test and train appropriately so that local church pastors and the congregation can affirm to send. Therefore, in our remaining time, I would like us to consider four specific ways we try to be deliberate about a process for Auburndale Baptist Church to be adequately informed to grant an external call in an individual's life, specifically these two families who sit here before us—one to be sent to the mission field, the other into the pastorate.

TESTING

We know from Paul that God gives some men to the church who are apostles, prophets, evangelists, pastors and teachers for the equipping and building up of the church (Eph. 4:11–12). The best way to find them is to test those who feel an internal calling to this work. The best way to test men for the office of pastor is through the qualifications for this office clearly mapped out for us in Scripture (1 Tim. 3:1–7; Titus 1:5–9). Through these listed characteristics, we can begin to determine whether a young man desiring this work is called, especially through testing his gift to preach and teach. This is a testing that is carried out visibly in many ways before the congregation.

For example, when we had twelve different men preach a psalm on Sunday evenings this past summer, that was not only an opportunity for them to serve our church, but it also acted as a way for their preaching gifts to be tested before the entire church. These brothers are also tested when they go and visit you in your home. Not only are they caring for you and the church in coming to see you, but they are also being tested in a pastoral way, regarding how patient, kind, gentle, peaceful, respectable, and self-controlled they are; these are all qualities Paul highlights (1 Tim. 3:1–7; Titus 1:5–9).

TRAINING

This is testing that becomes a little more deliberate. This stage is reached when the pastors of the church have, to some degree, identified gifts reflected from 1 Timothy 3:1–7 in a man who needs to be more deliberately tested and trained through practical experience. This is where a brother begins to play a more active role in the leadership of the church, by, for example, regularly teaching a class or preaching for a whole month on Sunday evenings. This is someone the pastors begin to trust, sending him to the hospital on his own or allowing him to become more exposed to the decisions and directions of the church. This is someone who is involved in evaluating the sermons and the services every week. In all these efforts, these brothers are being trained for ministry and the members of the church continue to be served, encouraged, and cared for through their efforts.

[Address missionary family], you have been in many of our homes and we have been in yours. We have had the joy of fellowship with you. You have served our church in so many ways. *[Both wives]*, you have cared for our children as you have faithfully cared for your own. You have modeled a Christ-like attitude through a very difficult family schedule. *[Husbands of both families]*, you have preached and taught God's Word to us. You have helped several people spiritually grow through your counseling efforts. You have helped lead our public gatherings and have used your pastoral experience to help the pastors think through some difficult issues.

However, as we fellowshipped together and served with you both, something else was happening—you were being tested and trained before our eyes for the work to which you felt called. In God's kind providence, he has allowed our church the joy of Christian fellowship with you through that time to put us in a place to affirm you.

Affirming

Once the pastors and leaders have had adequate time to test and train a brother pursuing this office, the time comes to either affirm him or not. If the pastors feel a brother has been qualified for this office, we then recommend him to the congregation, so that they can evaluate him also. Because much of this testing and training is carried out visibly before the people and with the people, members of the congregation have, hopefully, now been informed enough to make their own decision. This has resulted in very helpful fruitful discussions in our members' meetings. If there are no concerns about the pastors' recommendation, the church comes back after a month of praying to vote.

This affirmation can come in different ways. It may be an affirmation for a brother to serve as an assistant pastor here in our church. It may be an affirmation because someone is leaving to pursue a ministry position. It may be to affirm a couple who are going to the mission field. Regardless of the scenario, the decision to ordain a brother as a pastor or missionary is the final step before we send him with the full support and external call of Auburndale Baptist Church.

[Missionary family], I have had one-on-one meetings with you to discuss your marriage, family, school challenges, and struggles with sin. The pastors have discussed your situation on numerous occasions. We have had several public discussions about you at members' meetings. Yet you still sit here because in all those discussions, we as a church have felt convinced, though the road you face will be hard, that this is the work the Lord has for you.

[Pastor family], as a pastor of this congregation you have already been tested, trained, and affirmed. However, you sit here because this congregation has such confidence in you to face the unique challenges of the church you leave to pastor, because of the faithfulness you have shown as you faced the challenges of our church as a pastor of this congregation. In a few moments, we will do what the church in Antioch did (Acts 13:3)—we will lay hands on each of you and pray, sealing our affirmation of you to pursue these opportunities by God's grace.

SENDING

It can be a complicated and involved process to send a man out. Whether it is someone pursuing a pastorate or missions, as a church we are, in sending him out, committing to regularly pray for him, possibly give wisdom and pastoral oversight in where he should go, then be in regular contact with him while on the field. There may be a commitment that needs to be made from the church to financially support him, especially if he is going as a missionary to the field and must raise his own financial support. Sending is not the end of the process, but rather the beginning of a new commitment that we as a local church give those who have been called, tested, trained, affirmed, and sent out from among us.

Application for our church

As we consider our responsibility as a church, we need to realize that we each have a responsibility for our church to be faithful to the external call. If you are one who desires the work of a pastor or missionary, Paul says that you desire a fine work (1 Tim. 3:1). Yet your responsibility is not simply to rely on your internal call, but to place yourself under the authority of the local church and trust that God will work through the pastors and believers in this congregation to affirm your internal call with an external call.

If you are not someone feeling this call, then your responsibility is to do what so many of you do well as faithful church members. That is to invest and pour your lives into one another, so that when the time comes to possibly affirm, you are well informed. Come on Sunday evenings to hear these different brothers preach. Approach them afterwards and encourage them with what you thought they did well, and lovingly correct them where they can improve. Put your personal preferences aside regarding whom you like better as a preacher, and embrace the opportunity someone else gets. If we each play the part God has for us, we will be encouraged, our church will be built, we will guard the gospel more faithfully, and we will have a great faith in whatever God's will is for each opportunity we have as a local church to grant an external call.

In our world today, someone does not have to have an external call to go into the ministry. But in a church that requires this, in a church that sees the necessity, in a church that realizes what is at stake (Antioch), I submit to you, God is honored, and a biblically faithful church will be found with those who desire to conduct themselves according to God's design and purposes.

ENDNOTES

Preface

1 "Interview—Dr. Albert Mohler, Radio Host and Theologian," November 8, 2006, at: adrianwarnock.com.

Introduction

1 Charles Bridges, *The Christian Ministry: An Inquiry into the Causes of its Inefficiency* (Edinburgh: Banner of Truth, 1967), pp. 91–92.

Chapter 1

1 "Leader's Insight: Get-It-Done Leadership—6 Questions for Pastor and Leader Andy Stanley," May 28, 2007, at: christianitytoday.com/le/currenttrendscolumns/leadershipweekly/cln70528.html?start=2.

2 The outline given here is based on my outline in *Visit the Sick: Ministering God's Grace in Times of Illness* (Leominster: Day One, 2008), pp. 18–29.

3 The biblical office of the "pastor" is synonymous with the terms "elder," "overseer," and "bishop" throughout the New Testament and is the appointed shepherd of the New Testament church.

Chapter 2

1 Cited by Jim Cromarty, *King of the Cannibals: The Story of John G. Paton, Missionary to the New Hebrides* (Darlington: Evangelical Press, 1997), p. 65.

2 James Montgomery Boice, *Acts: An Expositional Commentary* (Grand Rapids, MI: Baker, 1997), p. 226.

Chapter 3

1 Titus 1:6–9 and 1 Peter 5:1–4 are also clear, complimentary passages describing these biblical qualifications, although 1 Timothy 3:1–7 will be the primary passage of focus for this chapter.

2 Richard Baxter and William Brown, (ed.), *The Reformed Pastor* (Edinburgh: Banner of Truth, 2001), p. 53.

3 C. H. Spurgeon, *Lectures to My Students* (Grand Rapids, MI: Zondervan, 1954), p. 26.

4 Ibid., pp. 26–27.

5 Cited in Michael A. G. Haykin, Roger D. Duke, and A. James Fuller, *Soldiers of Christ: Selections from the Writings of Basil Manly, Sr. and Basil Manly, Jr.* (Cape Coral, FL: Founders Press, 2009), pp. 175–176.

6 Spurgeon, *Lectures to My Students*, p. 26.

7 Roger Ellsworth in Thomas K. Ascol, (ed.), *Dear Timothy: Letters on Pastoral Ministry* (Cape Coral, FL: Founders Press, 2004), p. 272.

8 Cited in Haykin, Duke, and Fuller, *Soldiers of Christ*, p. 174.

9 David Dickson, and George Kennedy McFarland and Phillip Graham Ryken, (eds.), *The Elder and His Work* (Phillipsburg, NJ: P & R, 2004), pp. 30–31.

Chapter 4

1 J. L. Dagg, *Manual of Church Order* (Harrisonburg, VA: Gano Books, 1990), p. 248.

2 Traditional Protestantism defined a true church by "True preaching of the word; proper observance of the sacraments; and faithful exercise of church discipline." See Edmund P. Clowney, *The Church* (Downers Grove, IL: IVP, 1995), p. 101.

3 Cited in James M. Garretson, *Princeton and Preaching: Archibald Alexander and the Christian Ministry* (Carlisle, PA: Banner of Truth, 2005), p. 55.

4 Mark Dever, *Nine Marks of a Healthy Church* (Wheaton, IL: Crossway, 2000), p. 26

5 Dagg, *Manual of Church Order*, p. 274

Chapter 5

1 See Appendix 2.

2 A helpful example of this is found in Mark Dever and Paul Alexander, *The Deliberate Church: Building Your Ministry on the Gospel* (Wheaton, IL: Crossway, 2005), pp. 158–159.

3 Cited in Haykin, Duke, and Fuller, *Soldiers of Christ*, p. 174.

Chapter 6

1 Cited in Arnold Dallimore, *George Whitefield: The Life and Times of the Great Evangelist of the 18th Century Revival*, vol. i (Carlisle, PA: Banner of Truth, 2001), p. 549.

2 Ibid., p. 550.

3 Ibid.

Chapter 7

1 John Flavel, *The Character of a Complete Evangelical Pastor Drawn by Christ in The Works of John Flavel*, vol. vi (Carlisle: Banner of Truth, 1997), p. 579.

FOR FURTHER HELP AND INFORMATION

Books

Ascol, Thomas K., (ed.), *Dear Timothy: Letters on Pastoral Ministry* (Cape Coral, FL: Founders Press, 2004)

Baxter, Richard, and Brown, William, (ed.), *The Reformed Pastor* (Edinburgh: Banner of Truth, 2001)

Bridges, Charles, *The Christian Ministry: An Inquiry into the Causes of its Inefficiency* (Edinburgh: Banner of Truth, 1967)

Brown, Charles J., *The Ministry* (Edinburgh: Banner of Truth, 2006)

Dever, Mark, *By Whose Authority? Elders in Baptist Life* (Washington, DC: 9Marks, 2006)

——and Alexander, Paul, *The Deliberate Church: Building Your Ministry on the Gospel* (Wheaton, IL: Crossway, 2005)

Dickson, David, *The Elder and His Work* (Phillipsburg, NJ: P&R, 2004)

Haykin, Michael A. G., Duke, Roger D., and Fuller, A. James, *Soldiers of Christ: Selections from the Writings of Basil Manly, Sr. and Basil Manly, Jr.* (Cape Coral, FL: Founders Press, 2009)

James, John Angell, *An Earnest Ministry: The Want of the Times* (Edinburgh: Banner of Truth, 1996)

Prime, Derek, and Begg, Alistair, *On Being a Pastor: Understanding Our Calling and Work* (Chicago: Moody, 2004)

Spurgeon, C. H., *Lectures to My Students* (Grand Rapids, MI: Zondervan, 1954)

⟶ Test, train, affirm & send into ministry

Websites/blogs

The author has a blog called 'Practical Shepherding' that addresses practical issues about ministry from a biblical, theological, and pastoral perspective. Visit: briancroft.wordpress.com

Other useful blogs include:

- Thabiti Anyabwile's blog "Pure Church," now at: thegospelcoalition.org/blogs/thabitianyabwile
- C. J. Mahaney's blog, at: sovereigngraceministries.org/Blog
- Don Whitney's website: biblicalspirituality.org. In particular, see the article "The Call of God to Preach the Gospel" (in the "Ministry" section of "Articles").

About Day One:

Day One's threefold commitment:
- To be faithful to the Bible, God's inerrant, infallible Word;
- To be relevant to our modern generation;
- To be excellent in our publication standards.

I continue to be thankful for the publications of Day One. They are biblical; they have sound theology; and they are relevant to the issues at hand. The material is condensed and manageable while, at the same time, being complete—a challenging balance to find. We are happy in our ministry to make use of these excellent publications.

JOHN MACARTHUR, PASTOR-TEACHER, GRACE COMMUNITY CHURCH, CALIFORNIA

It is a great encouragement to see Day One making such excellent progress. Their publications are always biblical, accessible and attractively produced, with no compromise on quality. Long may their progress continue and increase!

JOHN BLANCHARD, AUTHOR, EVANGELIST AND APOLOGIST

Visit our web site for more information and
to request a free catalogue of our books.

www.dayone.co.uk

North American web site—
www.dayonebookstore.com

Also available

Counsel your flock
Fulfilling your role as a teaching shepherd

PAUL TAUTGES

96PP, PAPERBACK

ISBN 978-1-84625-154-2

The ministry of counseling has for too long been relegated to the professional counselor. Paul Tautges brings the biblical command for discipleship right back to the local church and to all believers. Rather than send people who are struggling spiritually, socially, and emotionally to a limited group of professionals, Tautges makes the case theologically that the responsibility for all church members is to disciple one another and to restore hurting people.

In this companion to his previous book, *Counsel One Another*, he makes it clear that for this one-another ministry to take place it is essential that pastors understand the key role that they play in the discipleship process. Believers need a way to measure their pastor's discipleship philosophy and skills and pastors need a way to teach them to be involved in the counseling, discipleship, restoring-one-another ministry.

'This book gets it right! Comprehensive and convincing, *Counsel Your Flock* shows how true biblical counseling and preaching fit hand-in-glove. Those who preach, teach, or counsel regularly are sure to benefit greatly from this helpful resource.'

DR. JOHN MACARTHUR, PASTOR-TEACHER OF GRACE COMMUNITY CHURCH IN SUN VALLEY, CALIFORNIA

'The ministry of counseling has for too long been relegated to the professional counselor. Paul Tautges brings the biblical command for discipleship right back to the local church and to all believers.

This is a book about local church discipleship, of which leadership is a big part. *Counsel Your Flock* addresses an important need. This is a must read!'

DR. RON ALLCHIN, EXECUTIVE DIRECTOR OF THE BIBLICAL COUNSELING CENTER IN ARLINGTON HEIGHTS, ILLINOIS

Also available

Comfort those who grieve
Ministering God's grace in times of loss

PAUL TAUTGES

144PP, PAPERBACK

ISBN 978-1-84625-155-9

Until the end of time, when the curse of sin is finally removed, suffering will be a large part of the human experience—and a large part of that suffering will be walking through the painful reality of death. Death is not foreign territory that ministers of grace walk upon. As a result, "Death," writes Paul Tautges, "provides a natural opportunity not only for ministry to others, but also for personal growth in ministers." Therefore, church shepherds must not waste these precious and painful occasions that God provides for the demonstration of mercy and the advantage of the gospel.

This book is a treasure chest of pastoral theology that will equip ministers to reach out to those who grieve with the Christ-centered comfort of God rooted in the gospel. The theological foundation espoused here, as well as the numerous practical helps that are included, will help any servant of the Lord to point the hearts and minds of the bereaved to the "man of sorrows" who is "acquainted with grief" (Isa. 53:3).

'Every minister of the gospel will find this book helpful. We are given concrete ideas for consoling those who are dying and then on preparing funeral messages which not only comfort the grieving, but also challenge the lost with a clear gospel message. I know of no book like *Comfort Those Who Grieve*. Most "how to" books are shallow and often devoid of deep theological content. This excellent book is an exception.'

CURTIS C. THOMAS, PASTOR FOR OVER FIFTY YEARS, BIBLE TEACHER, AND AUTHOR OF LIFE IN THE BODY

'Here is biblical, insightful, and practical advice regarding serving those who grieve. Written with the tenderness and understanding of a gentle pastor, this book will be a helpful manual for those who guide others through the valley of the shadow of death. I hope it gains wide distribution!'

DR. LES LOFQUIST, IFCA INTERNATIONAL EXECUTIVE DIRECTOR

Also Available

Visit the sick

Ministering God's grace in times of
illness

BRIAN CROFT

96PP, PAPERBACK

ISBN 978-1-84625-143-6

The demands of the twenty-first-
century have led to the neglect of
certain essential responsibilities in the
life of a Christian. One of those is the
visitation and care of the sick in our
congregations. This book is designed
to instruct and motivate pastors,
church leaders, and other care-giving
Christians through the counsel of our
heroes of church history, to recapture
the practice of visiting the sick. This
is accomplished by considering three
specific areas. First, is our commitment
to the theological as we consider how
to most effectively care for their souls.
Second, is our commitment to the
pastoral, which instructs us how to
proceed with wisdom and discernment
in the variety of circumstances we
will face. Third, is our commitment
to the practical so that the manner in
which we care for the sick will help,
not hinder our effort to communicate
biblical truth to them.

'Many younger pastors (and not so young
ones as well) have never received the sort of
very practical guidance which Brian Croft gives
in this book. It will now be a recommended
text in my Pastoral Ministries class.'

**RAY VAN NESTE, PH.D., ASSOCIATE
PROFESSOR OF CHRISTIAN STUDIES,
DIRECTOR, R. C. RYAN CENTER FOR
BIBLICAL STUDIES, UNION UNIVERSITY,
ELDER, CORNERSTONE COMMUNITY
CHURCH**

'Church member, let this book equip you to
become more useful to those in your church
who are ailing. Young pastor, gain from Brian's
practical wisdom. Seasoned pastor, let this
book remind you of the privilege it is to serve
and encourage the sick in a fallen world. I plan
to read it together with our elders, and hope
to make it available to our congregation as an
equipping tool.'

**PAUL ALEXANDER, SENIOR PASTOR, FOX
VALLEY BIBLE CHURCH, ST. CHARLES, IL,
CO-AUTHOR, THE DELIBERATE CHURCH**

Also available

Teach them to pray
Cultivating God-dependency
in your church

PAUL TAUTGES

128PP, PAPERBACK

ISBN 978-1-84625-196-2

A life of prayer is irrefutable proof of
God-dependency. This is true not only
of the individual believer, but also of
the local church, as evidenced in the
New Testament. Churches therefore
need to learn how to pray. But who
will teach them? In this book, Paul
Tautges convinces his readers that
teachers and church leaders must not
only tell their flocks to pray—they
must also teach them how to do it.
They must habitually instruct them in
the biblical principles, examples, and
commands concerning a life of prayer.
In short, churches need a biblical
theology of prayer. And leaders need
a practical tool to help them produce
an atmosphere of God-dependency in
their churches. *Teach Them to Pray* is
that tool.

'Paul Tautges not only encourages us to pray
corporately, but he also instructs us to pray
biblically. This book ... will prove valuable
to all members of a congregation. All of us
need encouragement and instruction in the
discipline of corporate prayer, and this book
will help us to that end.'

**JERRY BRIDGES, INTERNATIONAL SPEAKER
AND BEST-SELLING AUTHOR, *THE PURSUIT
OF HOLINESS***

'Use *Teach Them to Pray* as a springboard to
cultivate your own ideas on how you, as a
pastor or church leader, can cultivate prayer in
your church in our day of widespread
prayerlessness and spiritual amnesia.'

**DR. JOEL R. BEEKE, PRESIDENT, PURITAN
REFORMED THEOLOGICAL SEMINARY,
GRAND RAPIDS, MICHIGAN, USA**

Also available

Look after your voice

Taking care of the preacher's greatest asset

MIKE MELLOR

96PP, PAPERBACK

ISBN 978-1-84625-125-2

'As a hammer is to a carpenter, a scalpel to a surgeon, a trowel to a brick mason or a needle to a tailor—so the voice is to a preacher. Man's voice is the primary means God uses to deliver His Word to mankind, yet how often we who are called to impart the most important truths in the world are apt to neglect, if not wilfully abuse our all-vital 'tool of the trade'. Can there be any more pitiful sight in all nature than a God-sent preacher who is forced to be silent? We are not thinking here however of a silence brought about by pressure from ungodly sources, but that which has been enforced because of the preacher's own negligence concerning his voice. Mike Mellor's goal is not to produce another speech book (of which a good number can be found, usually aimed at actors or singers) but that something of our high calling as God's spokesmen may be re-kindled and as a consequence our desire to care for the frail vehicle God has designed to convey his Word may be increased.

'… I haven't seen anything like it for years, so it fits a good and helpful niche in the market … If, like me, you are prepared to pay the social cost of conditioning your voice by compulsive 'humming', you should still buy this little volume for the serious advice it contains.'

JONATHAN STEPHEN, PRINCIPAL, WALES EVANGELICAL SCHOOL OF THEOLOGY AND DIRECTOR, AFFINITY

'In much of our modern preaching, a great deal of catching up is necessary in terms of actual effective delivery. This book by an open-air preacher will help us in our public speaking—even if our voices never have quite the resonance of a John Chrysostom, a Whitefield or a Billy Graham. I certainly intend to put into prayerful practice the invaluable suggestions and exercises given us by Mike Mellor.'

RICO TICE, CO-AUTHOR OF CHRISTIANITY EXPLORED AND ASSOCIATE MINISTER AT ALL SOULS CHURCH, LONDON